# ADOLF HITLER

Liz Gogerly

W
FRANKLIN WATTS
LONDON • SYDNEY

**Maps** Ian Thompson
**Designer** Thomas Kee
**Editor** Louisa Sladen
**Art Director** Jonathan
**Editor-in-Chief** John C. Miles
**Picture Research** Susan Mennell

**Consultant** Eileen Yeo
Professor of Social and Cultural
History, University of Strathclyde

First published in 2002
by Franklin Watts
96 Leonard Street
London
EC2A 4XD

Franklin Watts Australia
56 O'Riordan Street
Alexandria
NSW 2015

ISBN 0 7496 4644 6

Dewey classification: 943.086

A CIP catalogue record
for this book is available
from the British Library.

Printed in Hong Kong/China

ewark's Pictures
Evans Picture
Library (main)
Back cover: Mary Evans Picture Library
AKG London pp. 25,36, 42-43, 59,
67,73, 79, 83, 96-97
Hoffmann Archive, Bavarian State
Library p. 39
Mary Evans Picture Library pp. 2, 3,
14, 28-29, 40, 54, 61, 77, 105
Peter Newark's Pictures pp. 7, 12-
13,16, 22, 32, 35, 45,46, 52, 56-57,
62, 64-65, 69, 71, 84, 89, 91, 92-93,
99,100-101
Popperfoto pp. 5, 8-9, 11, 18, 30, 49,
51, 63, 87
Franklin Watts (with thanks to the
Imperial War Museum, London)
pp. 76t, 76b

# Adolf Hitler
# 1889-1945

# Contents

# Introduction

**It has been over half a century since the death of Adolf Hitler, yet even now he has the power to fascinate and horrify us. New books about Hitler regularly make the bestseller lists.**

Photographs of him with his neatly trimmed moustache, and his ice-cold eyes turned to the camera, still send a chill down the spine. How can one man continue to create so much interest and so much fear?

History has had its fair share of evil characters, but Adolf Hitler is still considered by many to have been the most inhumane and dangerous of all. It was his hatred of communists, Jews and other minority groups that brought about the deaths of over six million people in Nazi concentration camps. And it was his lust for power that caused the Second World War. The nature of his evil is hard to comprehend, as is the blind devotion of the followers who acted on his orders.

As we search for answers we find contradictions in his character. Hitler was a man of culture who enjoyed paintings and the company of women and children. For a few years he brought prosperity and stability to Germany too. He was also the visionary behind Germany's great motorways and backed the development of the "people's car" (or VW Beetle, as we now know it). At the end of the war, when all hope had deserted him, this same man ordered that the very country he had tried to make so great should be destroyed. Can we ever understand such a man? As long as we keep trying, then there is always hope that history will not repeat itself, and that never again will the world be torn apart by the dreams and blind hatred of a single person.

## What's in a name?

**Adolf (male) German:** composed of the Germanic elements: adal, which means noble, and wolf, which, of course, means wolf. This form of the name was first introduced into Britain by the Normans, but it did not become at all common in Europe until the eighteenth century. The name's association with Adolf Hitler has meant that the name has hardly been used since the Second World War.

# The early years

**Throughout his life Hitler was secretive about his childhood. If people delved into his background he feared that they would uncover the madness that was in his family.**

They might even have found that he had Jewish blood; a fact that he could never disprove because his father had been illegitimate. Now, historians know that he didn't have a Jewish connection, but it's interesting that possibly one of the most anti-Semitic characters in history lived with that uncertainty. When Hitler wrote about his early life he claimed it had been poor and unhappy. In truth, Hitler's family were comfortably off, and, although his father was strict, his mother spoiled him.

## Mother love

Adolf Hitler was born on 20 April 1889 in Braunau-am-Inn, Austria. His father Alois was an arrogant, hard-drinking customs official with an eye for women. Hitler's mother, Klara, had been the household maid and became Alois's third wife in 1885. She was quiet and obedient, and looked after Alois's two other children from his previous marriages,

Alois and Angela. She bore her husband five more children but of these only Hitler and his younger sister Paula survived. Hitler was probably a normal healthy baby, but Klara feared she might lose another child so treated him as if he was sickly. She constantly fussed over him. Hitler's father was rarely at home so the bond with his mother grew stronger.

Life changed when Hitler was six. His father retired from the customs service. The family moved to a house with nine acres of farmland at Hafeld, near the town of Lambach. Suddenly, Hitler's drunken, domineering father was at home more often. He bullied and beat Klara and his eldest son, Alois. Despite the family traumas, Hitler looked back fondly on those years. Perhaps this was because he spent long hours in the fields surrounding the farm, playing his

▶ *Adolf Hitler as a baby and the notice of his birth in a local paper. His mother Klara fed him lots of cakes and biscuits to fatten him up.*

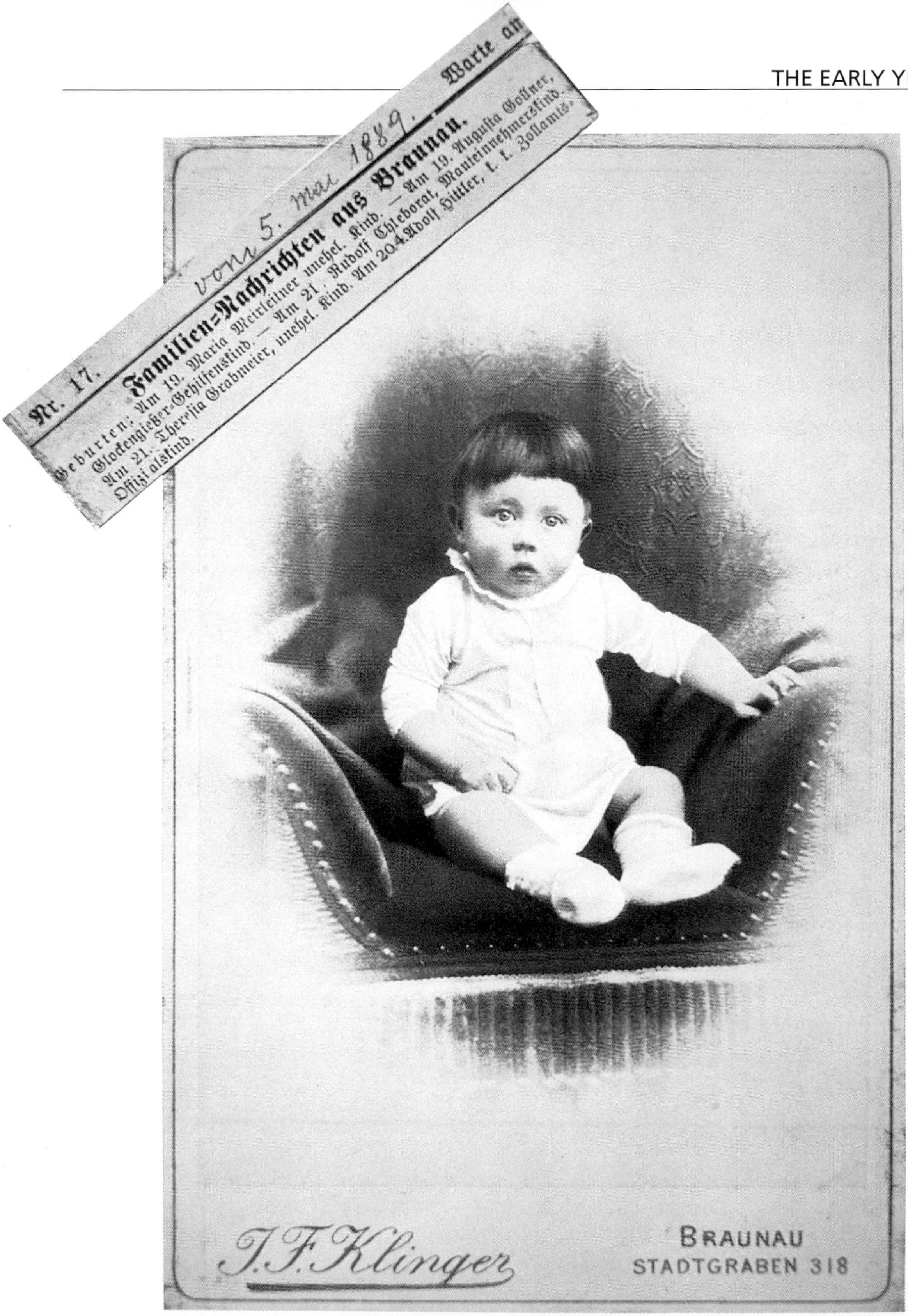
Nr. 17. vom 5. mai 1889. Warte a

**Familien-Nachrichten aus Braunau.**

Geburten: Am 19. Maria Meirleitner unehel. Kind. — Am 19. Augusta Gollner, Glockengießer-Gehilfenskind. — Am 21. Rudolf Chleborat, Mauteinnehmerskind. Am 21. Theresia Grabmeier, unehel. Kind. Am 20. Adolf Hittler, k. k. Zollamts-Offizialskind.

*◀ The ten-year-old Hitler (centre, top row) looks cocky and self-assured in this class photograph taken at the village school near Linz.*

favourite game of cowboys and Indians. He did quite well at school.

When Hitler was seven his brother Alois left home. From now on Hitler was forced to do more chores, which he hated. His father kept a critical eye on him. Months later, the family moved into the town of Lambach. Hitler missed the countryside, but he didn't miss working on the farm. He continued to do well at school, but his father now beat him. On one occasion, Alois hit Hitler so hard he thought that he had killed him. Early on, Hitler decided not to cry when his father attacked him. Gradually, he became more rebellious and rude to his father.

## War games

In 1899, the same year that the Hitler family moved to another new home near Linz, the Boer War broke out in South Africa. Hitler and his friends would recreate great battles between the Boers and the British. Hitler particularly enjoyed playing the part of the leader of the Boers – killing British soldiers. At other times, Hitler played more sadistic games. He'd sneak off to the local church-yard armed with his father's airgun, and take great pleasure in shooting rats.

## Paula Wolff (née Hitler)

In 1959, Paula Hitler confided to a British journalist: "The autobahn and the VW are probably the best things my brother left behind." At this time, Hitler's younger sister was living by herself under the assumed name of Frau Wolff in shabby attic rooms in Vienna. She worked as an assistant for an insurance company and kept herself to herself. As Hitler's only surviving full sibling she had become the object of much curiosity and was interrogated by the Allies after the war. During those interviews she showed genuine emotion towards her brother: "His end brought unspeakable sorrow to me," she admitted before breaking down in tears.

In truth, Hitler had not been a brilliant brother. He had turned his back on his mentally retarded sister when their mother Klara had died, and had only given over his portion of their father's pension to help with her upbringing when pressed upon by his relatives to do so. In between the years 1908 and 1921 she never saw her brother; at times she believed he was dead. When he eventually came back into her life it was on his terms. They would meet very rarely – not even as often as once a year. He never spoke or wrote about her, but it's said that he granted her a small allowance to keep her out of the limelight. She died in June 1960. The whereabouts of her grave, like so many other details of her life, remain a mystery.

## Teenage years

By the time Hitler was in his early teens, his school work had began to suffer. At secondary school in Linz he failed mathematics and natural history. His real talent was for drawing and he hoped to become an artist. He also became more interested in politics. In the early nineteenth century Austria had formed part of the German Confederation. Following the Franco-Prussian War of 1871, Austria had become part of the Habsburg Austro-Hungarian Empire. Meanwhile, other German-speaking territories had been united by Bismarck to form a great German empire. Hitler's father was a supporter of the Habsburgs while Hitler became more interested in German nationalism.

In January 1903, Hitler's father was drinking at a tavern when he died suddenly from a pleural haemorrhage. The tension at home lifted immediately but Hitler, who was now 14, remained stubborn and uncooperative at school. He eventually left school at 16 without a school-leaving certificate. With no father to bully him and a mother who allowed him to do as he pleased, Hitler was free to indulge in drawing, reading and listening

▲ A sketch of Hitler by a fellow pupil in secondary school. Hitler, who was 16 at the time, already has a small moustache.

the Academy of Fine Arts in Vienna. He'd visited the Austrian capital in 1906 and had been inspired by its architecture and culture. By September 1907, Hitler was on a train heading for Vienna – his dream was coming true.

## Disappointment and despair

Hitler's dreams soon fell flat when the Academy judged his test drawings to be unsatisfactory. They believed his talents lay in architecture. To become an architect, Hitler needed to attend a technical college. But he needed a school-leaving certificate for that. Hitler was still determined that he'd get into the Academy to study art.

For a few lonely weeks Hitler fretted about his future. At home, his mother was becoming seriously ill. At the end of October 1907, Hitler rushed back to Linz. By now Klara had been diagnosed with cancer and she only had months to live. Hitler spent the next two months at his mother's bedside. She died a few days before Christmas and Hitler sketched her body one last time. Overcome with grief, he spoke to nobody for days. It is said that Adolf Hitler never liked Christmas again.

to the operas of Richard Wagner. His mother, who had a widow's pension, didn't pressurize him to look for a job as was expected of most young men. When he was offered an apprenticeship as a baker Hitler turned his nose up – he had grander plans! He wanted to study art at

## Vienna

By February 1908, Hitler was back in Vienna. He had a small inheritance and a pension, but to make his money last he had to live frugally. He shared a tiny flea-ridden room with his best friend from school, a musician called Gustl Kubizek. Hitler spent most of his time practising his drawing and painting or reading. Sometimes he managed to get cheap seats at the opera and theatre. At least he felt he was living the life of an artist – although this young bohemian didn't drink, smoke or have girlfriends. In 1909 when he was 20, Hitler was rejected by the Academy again. By now his funds were running very low. He was poor, lonely and filled with self-pity, but he still refused to look for a job – in his heart he believed he was destined for higher things.

## Life on the streets

By October 1909 Hitler was living on the streets, sleeping in doorways and selling his few possessions to survive. When it got colder he slept where he could: on the floors of bars or cafes, in cramped and

▶ *This watercolour of an old courtyard in Munich was painted by Hitler in 1914. By this time he had accepted that his talent was for painting architecture.*

DER DRAHTZIEHER,

Kopf= u. Handarbeiter wählt:

 Völkischen Block

dirty labourers' barracks and cheap lodging-houses. He sold most of his clothes, including his overcoat, and finally took refuge at an asylum for the homeless in the suburb of Meidling. He was painfully thin and his blue eyes looked sad and empty. In 1910, he moved to a slightly more habitable hostel called the Männerheim. Its reading rooms and library provided Hitler with the intellectual stimulus he'd been missing.

## Political awakening

After a few months Hitler's strength returned, and with it came feelings of self-importance and confidence. At the Männerheim he became known for heading debates in the reading room. He directed months of frustration and anger at his own condition at the Jews and Marxists. At that time, Vienna was severely overcrowded, there was high unemployment and poverty. Many people blamed the large influx of immigrants, particularly Jews, for the worsening conditions. By 1910, Jewish people made up ten per cent of Vienna's population

◀ *This early Nazi propaganda poster portrays a Jewish business-man as "the wire-puller" who controls the workers by force.*

but a disproportionately high percentage of those worked in finance, medicine, law, the media and performing arts. There was a growing tide of resentment against the Jews in the city. Hitler became obsessed with the "Jewish problem". He believed the Jews controlled the economy and the arts and it was their fault that he had been denied success. As a child, Hitler had dreamed of a new German empire with Austria reunited with her fellow German-speaking nations. Once more, he found himself looking towards the "fatherland" and all things German.

## The boy becomes a man

In 1910, Hitler was rejected by the Academy again, and once more they suggested he try architecture. In the following years he continued to live at the Männerheim, spending his days painting and reading about politics, developing a profound understanding of the use of propaganda. By May 1913 he realized it was time to move on; he hoped to continue his studies in Munich. About to leave Vienna, he reflected upon his life so far: "I had set foot in this town while still half a boy and I left it a man, grown quiet and grave."

# The passionate soldier

**Munich was the capital of Bavaria, and in 1913 it was considered to be, after Paris, the cultural centre of continental Europe.**

Hitler felt immediately at home in Munich. But he steered clear of the lively culture that was based around people meeting in cafes and discussing politics and art. He rented a small room and spent much of his time painting architectural scenes which he very rarely managed to sell. Once again he found himself visiting libraries, but now he was reading about Marxism and its relation to the Jewish question. He talked of becoming a student at the Munich Art Academy but there's no evidence that he even applied. He was living a lonely, hand-to-mouth existence, seemingly without direction. Yet Hitler later claimed that he'd never been happier.

## A call to arms

On 18 January 1914, it seemed as if Hitler's plans to become an artist might be thwarted again. Late that afternoon the unexpected knock on his door from a German policeman was followed by a notice to sign up for military service at Linz in Austria. If he didn't leave to do so at once he might be arrested and thrown in prison. In February, Hitler reported for military duty at Salzburg in Austria, but a medical officer found him unfit for military service. Apparently years of poverty had left him weak and run-down. Hitler returned to Munich to continue his lonely existence. He couldn't have guessed how political events in Germany were about to explode and change the course of his life.

In June 1914 the Austrian heir to the throne, Archduke Franz Ferdinand, was assassinated by a Serbian terrorist in the city of Sarajevo. By August 1914, World War One had broken out with Austria and Germany at war with Russia, Britain and France.

◀ *An excited Hitler (circled) near the front of a crowd in Munich on 2 August 1914, the day after Germany declared war on Russia. The next day France joined the war against Germany and Hitler volunteered to fight.*

## At the Western front

When war fever gripped Germany, Adolf Hitler was infected too. Years later in his book, *Mein Kampf (My Struggle)* he said: "Even today I am not ashamed to say that, overcome with rapturous enthusiasm, I fell to my knees and thanked Heaven from an overflowing heart for granting me the good fortune of being allowed to live at this time." Hitler volunteered for action and this time he was accepted. By October 1914 he was at the Western Front fighting for the 16th Bavarian Reserve Infantry Regiment.

Hitler served as a regimental runner, a dangerous job that involved carrying messages and orders for officers through battlefields under fire. Fellow soldiers had mixed feelings about the young Austrian who preferred his own company, or that of a small white dog he'd named Fuchsl, and who didn't drink, smoke or talk about women. Some soldiers respected his intellectual air and the way he talked about art, architecture or politics. Others admired his bravery and leadership

◀ *Hitler (right) in 1916 with fellow soldiers Ernst Schmidt and Sergeant Max Amann. The little white dog is Fuchsl (little fox) which Hitler had taught circus tricks such as climbing ladders.*

qualities, while a few were unnerved by his excessive sense of duty. In every way he seemed different, and perhaps for this reason he was never promoted beyond the rank of corporal.

## A charmed life

Something else set Hitler apart from the other soldiers. He believed he was special and led a charmed life. On one occasion in the trenches he claimed he had heard a voice telling him to move. He did as he was bid and a few minutes later a shell hit the very spot he'd occupied previously. At other times he made strange prophecies about himself: "You will hear much about me," he told the other soldiers, "just wait until my time comes."

Hitler's bravery won him military honours; by December 1914 he'd won the Iron Cross, Second Class, for saving the life of an officer; towards the end of the war he collected the Iron Cross, First Class, for exemplary behaviour. In 1916 he was involved in the Battle of the Somme, but in October he was injured during a shell attack. He begged to stay at the front but was sent to a field hospital. In the following months he recuperated in hospitals near Berlin and in Munich.

Within a short time of being back in Munich, his anti-Semitism began to reignite, filling him with bitterness. This bitterness was made worse by his anger towards those who weren't fighting in the war, and the pacifists who were trying to stop it. His sense of German nationalism grew stronger still.

## A losing game

In March 1917, Hitler was relieved to be back at the front in Belgium with his fellow soldiers and his dog Fuchsl. In between action there were often quiet periods when he could get out his water-colours and paint battle scenes. There was also time to read up on politics, history and philosophy. He had difficult times too; in August, Fuchsl went missing and then his paintings were stolen. When food was short the regiment were forced to eat cats and dogs, but following Fuchsl's disappearance Hitler couldn't bring himself to eat dog meat.

In the mud and chaos of the trenches it was hard to determine who was winning the war. The casualties on both sides were enormous, but by August 1918 the Allies broke through the German lines at Amiens. In September Hitler's regiment was moved to Flanders and in October Hitler was involved in a mustard-gas attack. The effects of the gas could be deadly and sometimes even those who wore masks went blind. Hitler was one of the lucky ones; his blindness would only be temporary.

## A future in politics

In November 1918 Hitler was recovering in hospital when he heard that the German armistice had been signed. A German defeat was terrible but the effects of the war – the loss of two million German lives and a shattered German economy – made the blow even harder to bear. Hitler was devastated but made a pact with himself – if he recovered his sight then he would enter politics and forget about architecture. He later claimed he had a strange kind of vision, when he heard voices telling him to save Germany. He said that it seemed like a miracle when he suddenly found he could see again. Hitler wanted to feel that fate was pushing him towards a career in politics.

When Hitler was discharged from hospital in November 1918, Germany was in revolutionary turmoil. The war had caused terrible food shortages and Germans were angry with their leaders, especially their Kaiser, Wilhelm II, who had ruled as German emperor and King of Prussia since 1888. Wilhelm had dominated German politics until 1908 but in the following years illness had lessened his influence. By November 1918 mutinies in the army and navy and strikes by the workers had forced Wilhelm II to abdicate and flee to the Netherlands.

## The Weimar Republic

On 9 November a republic had been declared, and a coalition government of the Social Democrat Party, the Catholic Centre Party and the Democratic Party was formed by Friedrich Ebert, the leader of the Social Democrat Party. This would be Germany's first encounter with a democratic government but it would be beset with many problems. In early 1919 the new government met in Weimar to draw up its constitution. Ebert was appointed president of the new Weimar Republic but he would have a difficult time holding together a government composed of so many political factions The Republic also had many enemies.

It was hated by the German nationalists, the socialists and the communists. These were unstable times, and the threat of revolution was never far way. The communist uprising by the Bolsheviks in Russia in 1917 was a chill reminder of how bloody and cruel revolution could be, and in December 1918 the Germans were about to get their first taste of a "Red" uprising.

In Berlin, a communist group called the Spartacists had attempted, and nearly succeeded, in calling a revolution. Ebert was keen to crush such rebellion and employed a group of right-wing ex-soldiers called the Freikorps (free corps) to crush the revolt. The Freikorps succeeding in stamping out the Sparticists, and Ebert eventually gave them the responsibility of defending the Weimar Republic from further attempts at revolution. Although they were employed as peace-keepers, the Freikorps would prove to be a bloodthirsty mob. Their brutality only served to destabilize Germany even further. Opposition street armies, mainly composed of communists, soon gathered, and in a matter of months the country had become a dangerous place to live.

## The experience of war

Hitler responded to these events with anger. He blamed the situation on the enemies from within – Jews, Bolsheviks and those who believed in democracy. War had brought millions of ordinary Germans nothing but poverty. The Treaty of Versailles, which would officially end the war, took land away from Germany and was a terrible humiliation. But years later Hitler said: "If I weren't myself hardened by this experience, I would have been incapable of undertaking this Cyclopean task which the building of an empire means for a single man." After World War One most Germans craved peace, but Hitler wanted revenge.

▼ *During the communist Spartacist uprising in Berlin in 1919, members of the Freikorps crushed the opposition using armoured cars and flamethrowers.*

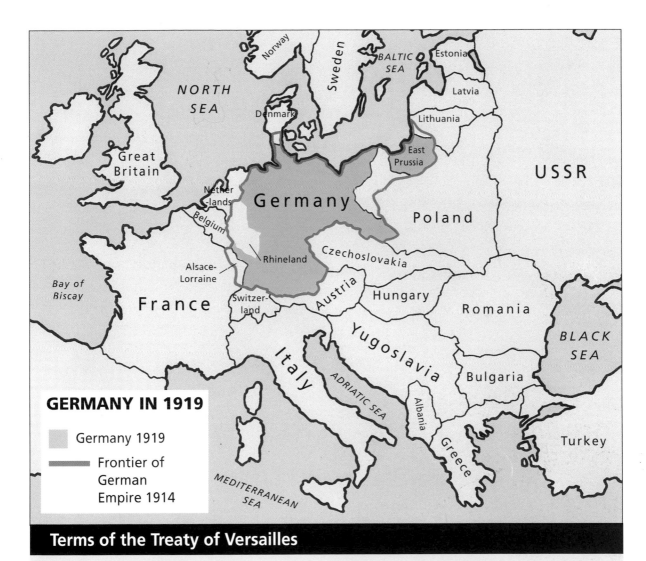

## GERMANY IN 1919

Germany 1919

Frontier of
German
Empire 1914

## Terms of the Treaty of Versailles

- Germany and its allies to take responsibility for causing World War One
- Germany to lose an equivalent of 13 per cent of its pre-war area: Alsace-Lorraine in the west to be given to France; part of Posen and West Prussia in the east to be handed to Poland
- Allied troops to occupy the Rhineland for at least five years
- A reduction of the German army to 100,000 men
- Germany to pay reparations for war damage; fixed at 132 billion gold marks (about £6,600,000,000 today)

# Hitler and the start of the Nazi Party

**When Hitler returned to Munich in December 1918, soldiers and workers had taken control in a rebellion and a Bavarian Republic had been proclaimed by the communists.**

To add insult to injury – from Hitler's point of view – the rebellion had been led by a Jewish left-wing socialist called Kurt Eisner. Unsure of his future, Hitler volunteered as a guard at a prisoner-of-war camp 96 kilometres away at Traunstein. While Hitler was away from Munich, Eisner was killed and a communist group proclaimed the German state of Bavaria a part of the Soviet Union. Hitler returned to the city in March and witnessed the bloody street battles in which the Freikorps crushed this communist uprising. Soon after, Hitler was employed by the army as a propaganda officer, to assess and monitor the revolutionary atmosphere prevalent in Munich.

## Effects of Versailles

In June 1919, the new German government was forced to sign the Treaty of Versailles. People had hoped that the Allies would look favourably upon Germany's new democratic government and that the terms of the treaty would be lenient but they were not (see box on p. 23). There was no room for negotiation: the Allies said that they would continue to wage war against Germany if the government didn't agree to the terms of the treaty. One of the greatest blows was the reparation payment. It was to cripple Germany's already shaky economy. Very soon, Germany was suffering from high unemployment and inflation. Millions of unemployed and disillusioned soldiers added to the general climate of misery and resentment. The crime rates soared as people struggled to survive.

## An opening in politics

In September 1919, Hitler was ordered by the army to spy on a small right-wing group called the German Workers' Party

▼ *After 1918, thousands of injured soldiers were forced to beg on the streets of Germany. Scenes like this made most Germans fear another war.*

(DAP). The group seemed badly organized yet it was fiercely nationalistic and blamed the Jews and communists for Germany's problems. At first, Hitler wasn't impressed, but he had been looking for a way into politics and perhaps this was a good opportunity. After his second visit to the party, he was offered a position organizing recruitment and propaganda. He accepted, and in October gathered an audience of over a hundred people for a meeting at which he spoke for 30 minutes. For the first time, he realized he had talent as a speaker. Within months the gatherings got larger, as students, shopkeepers and army officers crammed into the meetings held in beer halls. Most of those crowds had heard about a new and brilliant speaker – Adolf Hitler.

## The lone wolf

On 24 February 1920, 2,000 people were drawn to a meeting of the DAP. Hitler was going to read out the main points of the new party programme (see the box on p 27) which he had helped to compile. His speech lasted for nearly two and half hours, but the crowd was transfixed throughout. They cheered when he ranted and shouted about bringing down the Jewish threat. They listened carefully as he altered his pitch and quietly talked about the union of all Germans. They believed he was honest and, still more importantly, capable of liberating Germany. As he went through each point the audience cheered. Anyone who jeered was forcibly removed by a band of ex-army officers. From now on Hitler called himself "the wolf" – it would become his nickname amongst close friends, but he personally liked the name.

## A new image

Inspired by Adolf Hitler, the membership of the DAP increased steadily throughout 1920. The party changed its name to the Nationalsozialistische Deutsche Arbeiterpartei (National Socialist German Worker's Party) (NSDAP) or the Nazi Party, for short. With his flair for propaganda, Hitler set about making other changes. He chose red as the new party colour, a deliberate move to provoke the communists, as this was their party colour. He picked the swastika as the party's symbol. The swastika was already used by some of the Freikorps, and against a black, white and red background it made a simple and effective banner. Publicity material advertised all Nazi meetings. Flags and posters adorned the meeting halls. Party members wore swastikas on their armbands. At demonstrations, Hitler's army band marched and sang songs with rousing choruses of "Sieg Heil, Sieg Heil!" Nazism was on a roll and making its mark upon the political fabric of Bavaria.

## A campaign of terror

The party had other influential members such as the writer Dietrich Eckart. He helped Hitler with his poor grammar and improved his public-speaking techniques. He also introduced him to rich, influential people. Another important member was Captain Ernst Röhm, who brought with him loyal soldiers ready to create terror among the communists on the streets of Munich. This same fearsome army eventually evolved into the Sturm Abteilung (SA) or storm troopers.

Hitler's reign of terror and intimidation was set to begin and it was calculated and cruel. "Cruelty impresses," he claimed. "People need a good scare. They want to be afraid of something. They want somebody to make them afraid, someone

### Hitler's DAP manifesto

- We demand the union of all Germans in a Greater Germany
- We demand... the revocation of the peace treaties of Versailles and Saint-Germain
- We demand land and territory to feed our people and to settle our surplus population
- Only members of the nation may be citizens of the state. Only those of German blood, whatever their creed, may be members of the nation. Accordingly no Jew may be a member of the nation

to whom they can submit with a shudder. Haven't you noticed, after a brawl at a meeting, that the ones who get beaten up are the first to apply for membership of the party?"

## The leader

By July 1921, Hitler's extraordinary ability to rouse a crowd had made him one of the leaders of the Nazi Party. The Nazis were fast becoming one of the largest nationalist parties in Bavaria. Party membership had increased to 6,000 by early 1922 and at a rally in Munich in

November 1922 there were 50,000 people in the crowd. In January 1923, at the time of the First Reich party rally, there were 20,000 members: a figure which rose to 55,000 by the end of the year. Although the party represented all classes, most of its membership was made up of social groups such as skilled craftsmen, civil servants and students. Hitler also realized the importance of friends in high places. He was now a guest in respected households such as the Wagners, the esteemed relatives of Hitler's favourite composer.

## Germany in crisis

For Germany, 1923 had been a terrible year. In January, following late reparation payments, French troops had occupied the Ruhr, Germany's most important industrial region. As a result the mark had plummeted, there had been enormous inflation, and unemployment had risen. Suddenly, the middle-classes saw the value of their savings slump and the working man couldn't feed his family.

▶ *The artist H.G. Boyer captures the intensity of Adolf Hitler at a Nazi meeting, circa 1922. In his neat suits, Hitler looked the picture of respectability but he was quite prepared to use force.*

▶ *Hitler takes to the snowy streets of Munich in 1923. He rarely missed the opportunity to promote the Nazi Party.*

Communist revolts in Saxony, Thuringia and Hamburg made people believe there could be a communist revolution throughout Germany. Hitler believed the time was right for a national revolution or Putsch (purge). The plan was to overthrow the Bavarian government, then force them to join the Nazis in a march on Berlin and impose a Nazi regime throughout the whole of Germany. In Italy the Fascist leader Benito Mussolini had staged a similar coup in 1922 and Hitler had very much admired his style.

## The Beer Hall Putsch

The plan was put into action on 8 November 1923. Hitler ordered the meeting of the Bavarian government at a beer hall called the Bürgerbräukeller to be surrounded by 600 storm troopers. With a gun in his hand, Hitler took the stage and proclaimed that the national revolution had begun. Members of the Bavarian government were seized and persuaded to support the plan.

In many ways the Putsch was badly organized – after seizing the government leaders, Hitler then allowed them to go free. This was a foolish decision that gave the leaders time to gather the army and police and put a stop to the coup. The next day, when 2,000 storm troopers attempted to enter Munich, there were street battles in which 16 Nazis were killed. Hitler was also injured but he managed to run away and hide at the home of his friends, the Hanfstaengls. At first Hitler believed he'd been shot but his injury turned out to be a dislocated arm. That evening, Hitler suffered pain and humiliation and even considered suicide. Helene Hanfstaengl, his friend and supporter, hid his revolver. She told him to continue with his struggle.

### Hitler's views, in his own words

*"What we must fight for is to safeguard the existence and reproduction of our race and our people, the sustenance of our children and the purity of our blood, the freedom and independence of the fatherland, so that our people may mature for the fulfilment of the mission allotted by the creator of the universe."*

"The cleanliness of this people [the Jews], moral and otherwise, I must say, is a point in itself. By their very exterior you could tell that these were no lovers of water, and, to your distress, you often knew it with your eyes closed. Later I often grew sick to my stomach from the smell of the kaftan-wearers. Added to this, there was their unclean dress and their generally unheroic appearance."

"If, with the help of his Marxist creed, the Jew is victorious over the other peoples of the world, his crown will be the funeral wreath of humanity and this planet will, as it did thousands of years ago, move through the ether devoid of men ... Hence today I believe that I am acting in accordance with the will of the Almighty Creator: *by defending myself against the Jew, I am fighting for the work of the Lord."*

## Behind bars

Hitler was arrested the next morning and taken to Landsberg Prison. He would be charged with high treason and sentenced to five years in prison. Humiliated and dejected by the defeat, Hitler went on hunger strike for two weeks. Eventually he was persuaded that the failure of the Putsch had been a good thing as people's enthusiasm had been stirred. When the revolution came it would require a leader, he was told, and that leader would be Adolf Hitler.

Life at Landsberg was comfortable and Hitler was treated well. He was exempt from manual work and allowed visitors. He mixed freely with other Nazis. He was also allowed books so he spent hours reading Nietzsche and Marx. However, the greatest luxury was having the time to write about his life. These memoirs, later published as *Mein Kampf*, revealed how passionately he hated the Jews and the communists, and how he would strive to make Germany great again.

▶ *Hitler looking defiant as he stands trial for his part in the Beer Hall Putsch. He stands between Ernst Röhm (front right) and General Ludendorff.*

# Building the Nazi Party: 1925–1929

**Hitler was released early from prison in December 1924. He had served little over a year of his sentence, but it had been time to gather his thoughts and assess the future of the Nazi Party.**

He realized he had work to do as many people had turned their backs on the party and membership was now less than 28,000. Realistic about the problems ahead, Hitler told his secretary Rudolf Hess: "I shall need five years before the movement is on top again." In many ways the political situation in Germany didn't favour Hitler's return to power. With the help of foreign loans, primarily from the USA, the dark days of 1923 seemed to have lifted. Money had been poured back into industry, there were more jobs and the German economy was looking healthier. To gain a foothold in politics, Hitler decided to change his tactics. The Jewish issue would be downplayed; instead he would concentrate on organization and policy. Rather than overthrowing the government, he would have to work within the government framework and win seats in the Reichstag (the German parliament).

## A new beginning

Hitler made his re-entry into public life on 27 February 1925. For dramatic effect he chose the Bürgerbräukeller – the scene of the disastrous Putsch – for his first public speech. Over 4,000 people jammed into the beer hall and a further thousand were turned away. As he walked towards the stage, the crowd cheered, women started to cry and men pushed forward to congratulate him. For two hours Hitler held the audience's attention. He demanded solidarity within the party but he told them that he could only do this if he was the undisputed leader of the Nazis.

▶ *Hitler poses for a photograph as he is released from Landsberg prison in 1924.*

If he was in charge, he reasoned, then he would take responsibility for leading the party to greatness.

## Winning back control

In fact it would take Hitler until 1926 officially to win back control of the party: after that time he was called *Führer* (leader) at all times. In the meantime, his comeback had not gone unnoticed by the Bavarian government. They quickly banned him from speaking in public, a boycott that was later extended to the states of Prussia, Saxony, Baden and Hamburg. Undeterred, Hitler spoke at closed meetings in front of wealthier supporters, while concentrating upon measures to build the Nazi Party. In 1925 the party was the smallest in Germany, but Hitler could appeal to all kinds of supporters. He could turn to the working man, and tell him that he too had worked as a labourer on building sites. At the same time, his artistic background meant that he could appeal to bohemians. In his speeches he would almost hypnotize the audience, using powerful rhetoric,

◀ *A portrait of Hitler signed by him on 28 April 1924 while he was still a prisoner. He's also written, " Erst recht!" ("Now I'll show you!").*

repeating his simple ideas over and over again. He told people the things they wanted to hear and he restored their confidence by telling them that Germany's problems were not their fault but those of Jews and communists. He appealed to people's sense of patriotism and told them the way forward for the German people was to restore one race – the Aryans – to Germany.

When *Mein Kampf* was published in July 1925 its high sales were a sign of Hitler's growing popularity.

## A vision for the future

In the following years Hitler set about reorganizing the party and creating departments for industry, agriculture, economy, foreign policy and publicity. The SS (Schutzstaffen) guard detachment were recruited to act as personal bodyguards to Hitler and the other Nazi leaders. The SA was reformed. Hitler Youth, the Women's League, and the Leagues of Nazi Lawyers, Nazi Doctors and Nazi Teachers were all launched. When the party held its first rally in Thuringia, the crowd used the raised-arm Nazi salute for the first time. By the end of 1926, membership was back up to 50,000.

## Behind the public face

Much has been written about Hitler since his death, as authors attempt to make sense of possibly the most evil man in history. In many ways Hitler was a straightforward man with simple tastes. He continued to live in cheap rented accommodation until 1927, when he rented a villa in Obersalzberg on the German-Austrian border as a place to relax at weekends. He enjoyed outdoor living and was never happier than when walking in the hills wearing lederhosen, a part of the traditional German dress. One of his early extravagances was a brand-new red Mercedes which he enjoyed driving to picnics in the woods and lakes outside Munich. Some of the picnickers enjoyed a swim, but Hitler refused to undress in front of the others and would usually read a book.

## "Uncle Alf"

Hitler genuinely enjoyed the company of women and children. He also loved dogs, but his sadistic streak was never far from the surface as he regularly threatened his animals with whips. Hitler was particularly secretive about his love life – probably because he seemed to prefer

the company of younger women. The relationship with his niece Geli Raubal was perhaps his most passionate but historians cannot agree how intimate the relationship actually was. Hitler was in his late thirties when his fun-loving nineteen-year-old niece caught his eye.

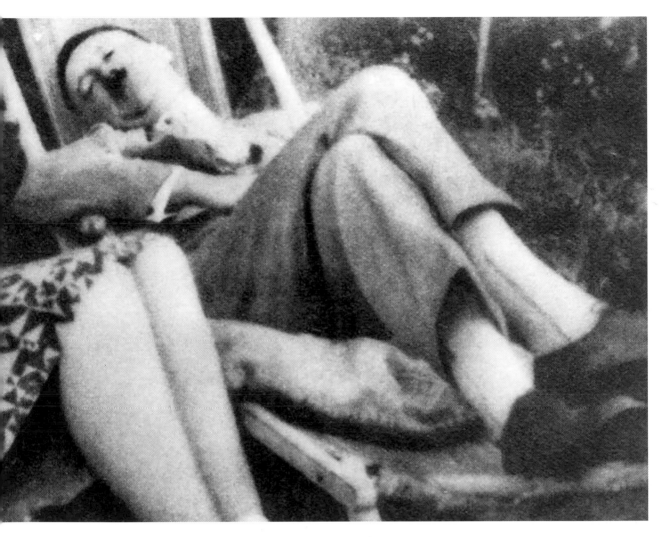

Geli was the daughter of his half-sister
Angela. The relationship between Hitler
and Geli began when Geli's mother
became housekeeper of his villa in
Obersalzberg. In 1927, Geli moved to
Munich to be near Hitler. For the next
few years she accompanied him to the

▲ *"Uncle Alf" and his niece Geli share a quiet
moment. Not much is known about Hitler's taste in
women, but Ernst Röhm once suggested that Hitler
was partial to peasant girls with large round bottoms.*

39

▲ Following the Wall Street Crash scenes of poverty and hardship became common in Germany. This photograph shows people queueing for soup outside the Salvation Army in Berlin in 1931.

theatre and opera and even to a few Nazi Party events. She loved it when "Uncle Alf" mimicked people, something he was good at, and he found her company relaxing.

Throughout this period the German economy had been growing. By 1928 the national income was 12 per cent higher than it had been in 1913. In his speeches Hitler claimed that he alone could save Germany, but what was he actually saving Germany from? Hitler was beginning to sound out of touch, something that was reflected in the poor results for the Nazi Party in the 1928 elections for the Reichstag. So Hitler continued to work at restructuring the party; in January 1929 he recruited Heinrich Himmler as the leader of the SS, and put him in charge of building an army of elite soldiers.

From October 1928 to September 1929 the membership of the party rose from 100,000 to 150,000, and in August 1929 the Nazis held their biggest rally yet at Nuremberg. Special trains transported party members to take part in the event and during one of the many spectacular parades, 60,000 storm troopers waving Nazi banners marched past Hitler. It took three hours for the parade to finish.

## The Depression hits

In September 1929, Hitler and Geli moved into a luxurious flat in Munich. "Uncle Alf" would prove to be a jealous and possessive lover who wanted to know how Geli spent each day. Meanwhile he was romancing another young woman called Eva Braun. Eva was a fresh-faced eighteen-year-old who worked in a photography shop. Hitler would take her on dates during the day in order to keep the liaison secret from Geli. For a while, Hitler's private life infuriated Nazi Party members as it seemed to take over from his political responsibilities. However, in October 1929, events in the USA were about to change the lives of everyone in Germany – including Hitler's. The Wall Street Crash on "Black Thursday" heralded an end to the new prosperity and when the USA called in loans they had made to Germany in the early 1920s, businesses began to fail. Unemployment rocketed and Germany was plunged into depression. This climate of desperation would make the perfect setting for the rise of Adolf Hitler and his Nazi Party.

# Creating the Third Reich

**Between 1928 and 1930 Germany's unemployment rose from about one million to over 3 million.**

The Weimar Republic eventually broke up in 1930 and Heinrich Brüning of the Centre party was made Chancellor (the equivalent to Prime Minister). The situation did not improve and people still looked for a new political figure, one who could steer the country back to prosperity. Hitler sensed imminent success. That August he told his colleagues that he expected a breakthrough within a year. In his speeches Hitler gave Germans the hope of a brighter future. He called for an end to democracy and offered a unified and stable government in its place. He spoke out against the Treaty of Versailles and denounced the reparation payments. He railed against the Jews and the communists and blamed them for Germany's problems.

▼ Hitler appears calm and relaxed as an adoring crowd of SA and other onlookers surround him in Munich, circa 1930.

He made promises he couldn't hope to keep, but in doing so he appealed to a wider spectrum of voters including farmers, workers, middle-class intellectuals and industrialists. By September 1930, the Nazis had gained 107 seats in the Reichstag and had become the second largest party in parliament.

## Personal tragedy

Behind the scenes, Hitler's life wasn't quite so triumphant. His work took him away from home a great deal and his relationship with Geli became strained. The affair ended in tragedy in 1931 when Geli was found, shot dead, in the flat. The verdict was recorded as suicide, but some people suggest that Hitler had killed her because she had taken another lover. We will never know the truth, but Hitler never forgot her and her photograph remained by his bed for the rest of his life.

In 1932 unemployment in Germany hit six million and industrial production was half that of 1928. In the presidential elections in May that year Hitler stood against the respected war hero, General von Hindenburg. Hitler was defeated but still gained 30 per cent of the votes.

Hitler's popularity was undeniable and certain politicians invited Hitler to join the coalition. But years earlier Hitler had promised himself that the Nazis would never be part of a coalition, and only he would be leader of the government. His steadfast belief in himself paid off. In the September elections of 1932 the Nazis took 230 seats and became the largest party in the Reichstag. Despite losing 34 of those seats in a second bout of elections in November, Hitler still refused to join the coalition. By now Hitler spent little time in Munich as his work was on the road, touring the country and preaching Nazism to an adoring public. Hindenburg had always distrusted Hitler. But in January 1933, in the face of Hitler's growing popularity, he appointed Hitler as Chancellor. He believed that if Hitler led a Nazi-Nationalist coalition government, with a cabinet which had a majority of Nationalists in it, then Hitler could be kept under control. It was a massive underestimation of Hitler's power and determination. Now that Hitler was Chancellor he aimed to secure complete control of the country.

▶ *An election poster from 1932 featuring von Hindenburg and Hitler.*

„Nimmer
wird das Reich
zerstöret —
wenn ihr einig
seid und treu"

1
Nationalsozialisten

## Determination and fire

One of Hitler's first moves as Chancellor was to apply for another election in March 1933. He hoped for a Nazi Party majority. That way he'd be even closer to his dream of creating a dictatorship. Within weeks he also gave the SA and the SS more power to deal with those considered enemies of the Nazis. Jews, communists and rival politicians were arrested, tortured and sometimes murdered. Hitler was hell-bent on success. When the Reichstag building caught fire on 27 February 1933 he blamed a Dutch communist, and in turn all communists. In truth, the fire was probably started by the Nazis to gain support in the upcoming election and also to enable them to pass emergency laws that would help them to crush the communists.

These new laws effectively legalized the reign of terror the Nazis were about to unleash. Now the police could arrest and hold people indefinitely, as well as censor post and make searches of people's houses. In the next few months it is

*Women seemed to adore Hitler. On a few occasions teenage girls threw themselves under his car, hoping that he might comfort them afterwards.*

estimated that about 25,000 people were arrested by Hitler's henchmen, the SA and SS. With the rights of the press withheld, and the right to hold public meetings curtailed, the Nazis were removing any opposition. Only the Nazis and Nationalists could campaign freely for election. But in March 1933 the Nazis still only managed to win 288 seats – which was 44 per cent of the votes. Hitler had anticipated a bigger majority but his plans for imposing total Nazi rule on Germany were still on track.

## Complete control

That same month the Reichstag passed the Enabling Law. It would give Hitler full dictatorial powers for four years. Now Hitler could establish a one-party system, with the Nazis in Berlin in complete control. With hindsight it's easy to ask why Hitler was given such free passage to the top, but the Nazis' reign of terror cannot be underestimated. On the day the Reichstag voted for the Enabling Law the building was surrounded by the SA, and Hitler had crushed much of the opposition. We must also remember Hitler's uncanny ability to sway people with his false promises, something that he continued to do throughout his leadership. Within months of taking power, Hitler had banned trade unions and replaced them by the German Labour Front. It was just one example of how Hitler would court a group to win their support, then completely betray them at the last minute.

Hitler moved quickly to establish Nazi rule across Germany. He placed his most loyal supporters in top-ranking positions. He chose Joseph Goebbels as his Minister of Propaganda and Hermann Goering as Prussian Minister of the Interior – both men would be key players throughout the existence of the Nazi regime. By a process called Gleichschaltung (co-ordination) all public groups were brought under Nazi control. Now teachers had to join the National Socialist Teachers' Organization, while all German employers had to join the Estate of German Industry. By July 1933, the last of the rival political parties, including the Nationalists, had been shut down. With effective manipulation of the media, Goebbels ensured that the only way forward for millions of Germans was Nazism. Towards the end of 1933 only the ageing President, Hindenburg, the army and the Catholic Church were not controlled by Hitler and the Nazis.

## The "Night of the Long Knives"

The only real threat to Hitler came from the SA. It now had over a million members. The fear and intimidation meted out by the SA, under the leadership of Hitler's old friend Ernst Röhm, had been instrumental in Hitler's rise to power. Now Hitler needed more support from Germany's middle classes, its leading industrialists and the army. To gain a larger foothold in these camps he needed to clean up his image and distance himself from the SA. On 30 June 1934, in an act of ruthless treachery, Hitler had 150 SA leaders, including Röhm, murdered by the SS. Perhaps as many as a thousand others were killed during a bloody night of terror known as the "Night of the Long Knives". The army leaders were pleased with Hitler's treatment of the unruly SA. When Hindenburg died on 2 August 1934 Hitler was declared Chancellor and President. From now on Hitler demanded that he be called Führer at all times.

▶ *Hitler addresses a Nazi rally in the 1930s. Such events were well rehearsed so they appeared perfect. Behind the scenes the SA were not so orderly.*

# Domestic policy – propaganda and the dictator

**If you had been alive in Nazi Germany during the 1930s you would have been bombarded by Nazi propaganda and expected to follow the party religiously.**

Posters and pictures showed Hitler as an all-powerful dictator, often making him look bigger and more handsome than he actually was. Everybody was expected to obey their Führer. To show their support people had to hang swastikas in their windows and greet each other with "Heil Hitler". Wardens were employed on each neighbourhood block to keep an eye on people and report those who didn't obviously show their allegiance to the Nazis. Everybody was being watched. There was a real fear that if you didn't support the party fully, then neighbours, or even your children, would inform the authorities. Once more fear was used as a key tool, and it became extremely difficult to rebel against the Nazis.

## The 1936 Olympic Games

The Nazis couldn't have maintained their control through terror alone. After defeat in war, depression, and years of political upheaval the Nazis offered German people a sense of pride and even a chance to have fun. Parades and celebrations of key dates in the Nazi calendar (see the table on p.53) were opportunities for people to gather together, sing and dance and generally forget about the bad times. They were, of course, carefully organized events designed to show off the new regime and allow Hitler to speak to his people. Most occasions were filmed or recorded for the radio. Perhaps the greatest of these Nazi extravaganzas was the 1936 Olympic Games in Berlin.

▲ *The black athlete Jesse Owens wins one of his four gold medals at the Berlin Olympic Games in 1936.*

Hitler was proud to show off his dynamic new country to an international audience. Germany scooped most of the medals, but when the black American sprinter Jesse James Owens won four gold medals, Hitler was said to be so angry he left the stadium rather than congratulate him. It was an early indication of how Germany's leader was really thinking.

The Nazis gave the impression of organization and efficiency, but in truth the administration was in a mess. All decisions were made by Hitler, but in running his government, he adopted a divide and rule strategy. He'd assign the same task to different people or offices and in doing so he would deliberately play people off against each other in order to safeguard his own position as master of the party. In that way, he could claim that without him it would all fall apart.

## The visionary

Despite their lack of organization, the Nazis were successful. Between 1933 and 1939 the German economy was recovering and unemployment fell to

◀ *Hitler launches the beetle-shaped Volkswagen in 1939. The car would become popular throughout the world after World War Two.*

### Calendar of Nazi celebrations

- **30 January** Hitler's appointment as Chancellor
- **24 February** Refounding of the party in 1925
- **24 March** Heroes' Remembrance Day for war heroes
- **20 April** Hitler's Birthday
- **1 May** National Day of Labour
- **2nd Sunday in May** Mothering Sunday
- **June** Summer Solstice
- **September** Nuremberg Party Rally
- **1 October** Harvest Thanksgiving
- **9 November** Anniversary of the 1923 Putsch in Munich

below one million. This recovery was partly because the world economy had improved, but it was also because Hitler had invested heavily in industry and rearmament. Naturally, in his speeches Hitler highlighted his own part in the new prosperity, but in some ways Hitler was a visionary. He masterminded the construction of canals, motorways and mass housing. It was his dream that one day every German would have a reliable car to drive on the new fast motorways.

Within a short time Hitler had brought a sense of stability to many Germans.

People could support their families and self-worth was restored. But behind all this success was a long-term goal. In 1936 Hitler hatched his Four Year Plan in which he stated his aims: to make Germany self-sufficient in food and raw materials, and prepare its armed forces in anticipation of war within four years.

## Persecution of the Jews

In 1933 there were about 500,000 Jews living in Germany. They made up less than one per cent of the population yet the Nazis blamed them for all of Germany's misfortunes. For years Hitler had raged against the Jews. He had likened them to germs that poisoned pure German blood. He looked forward to the day when Germans would become a racially pure race – the Aryans.

Now, as Führer, Hitler was in a position to pass many of his long planned anti-Jewish policies. Within months of becoming Chancellor, the SA were ransacking Jewish properties, arresting Jews, and sending them to concentration

◀ *A Jewish synagogue is destroyed on Kristallnacht. Such images provoked outrage abroad, and people finally began to question what was happening in Nazi Germany.*

camps. Then, on 30 March 1933, Hitler ordered a one-day boycott of Jewish shops and businesses. When foreign powers threatened to boycott Germany, Hitler realized he would need to tread carefully. However, he soon managed to introduce new laws to whittle away at Jewish liberties. To start with, Jews were expelled from the civil service and media, then they were banned from higher education. In 1935 the Nuremberg Laws stripped them of German citizenship, and marriages between Jews and people of German blood were forbidden.

## Kristallnacht

In 1938 life got even harder for the Jews. On 9–10 November 1938, the Nazis staged Kristallnacht (Night of the Broken Glass). The Nazis burned down about 200 synagogues and smashed and looted Jewish businesses and homes. Over 20,000 Jews were arrested and taken to concentration camps, and about 90 Jews were killed. By September 1939, nearly half of Germany's Jews had emigrated to other parts of Europe or the US. Many believed they were escaping to a better life; but they were actually running for their lives.

## Brainwashing the children

At Nuremberg in 1935 Hitler told the crowd of Hitler Youth that they were to be, "Fast as a greyhound, tough as leather, and hard as Krupp Steel." In these words he had encapsulated the Nazi philosophy of strength and racial superiority. He'd also struck at the hearts of those he believed to be the future of Germany – its children. Hitler always maintained that education was the only means of creating good Nazis. So schools and colleges were brought under Nazi control and the school curriculum carefully tailored. Subjects like biology could be used to promote racial superiority, while history could teach of Germany's great past. Foreign languages were dropped and replaced by character training in loyalty, obedience, courage and sacrifice. Physical training played its part too, in creating a stronger and healthier nation. Even though Hitler did not play any sport himself he placed great emphasis on games and physical fitness.

In 1926 Hitler started the Hitler Youth movement. By 1933 all other youth movements had been merged under its banner and by 1934 there were over 3.5 million members. Towards the end of the 1930s all children aged between ten and

▶ *When young boys became members of Hitler Youth they were given a dagger engraved with the words: "Blood and Honour".*

eighteen were expected to join; membership had risen to about 7 million. There were penalties for those who refused to join, but most children were happy to participate in a group that played sports and games and sang rousing anthems and brought them closer to their beloved Führer.

# Hitler the man – his private life

**As he became more powerful, Hitler distanced himself from other leading Nazis, but he still liked to surround himself with beautiful women.**

In early 1932 Hitler took Eva Braun as his mistress. It was an unusual affair, as Eva never appeared with him in public, while in private he was domineering and cold, banning her from dancing and smoking. Perhaps his enduring love for Geli meant he didn't have much more to give. It must have infuriated Eva that Hitler had kept Geli's room as it was when she was alive, and that he had fresh flowers placed there each week. In a desperate attempt to attract Hitler's attention, Eva attempted suicide, both in 1932 and in 1935 – but he continued to neglect her. In 1932 Hitler met Magda Quandt. He thought he'd found a woman he could marry. The fact that she was Goebbels' mistress didn't deter him, but when she did eventually marry Goebbels, he didn't seem too troubled by her loss. There were rumours of many other mistresses as well. But in truth Hitler probably just liked the attention and company of beautiful actresses and singers, rather than wanting a close relationship with any of them.

## The summer home

By the end of 1936 Hitler was spending a lot of time in the Austrian Alps, at his new summer retreat in the Berchtesgaden, the Berghof. The house had been developed on the site of his old villa, and though Hitler liked to portray himself as a man of simple tastes his new home revealed a more extravagant side to his nature. He collected Persian carpets, rare tapestries and fine art, and dinner was served on beautiful Dresden china with silver cutlery. There were fourteen bedrooms for guests, each supplied with a

▶ *Hitler poses for a photograph with Eva Braun and her niece in about 1937. Not many people knew that Hitler had a mistress until the end of the war.*

portrait of Hitler and a copy of *Mein Kampf*. Hitler held conferences there, but he also enjoyed entertaining. It was an honour to be invited to the Berghof, but all guests were aware of the strict rules (see the table below).

## The bohemian

In his youth Hitler had fancied himself as an artist, and a touch of the bohemian remained with him throughout his life. In his Vienna days he had devoured books about politics, but as he got older he

---

**Some of Hitler's instructions to guests at the Berghof, 1938**

- Smoking is forbidden, except in this bedroom
- At all times the Führer must be addressed and spoken of as such and never as "Herr Hitler" or other title
- Women guests are forbidden to use excessive cosmetics and must on no account use colouring materials on their fingernails
- Guests must present themselves for meals within two minutes of the announcing bell. No one may sit at table or leave the table until the Führer has sat or left
- Guests must retire to their rooms at 11 p.m. unless expressly asked to remain by the Führer

---

turned to literature. He rarely read German books, his tastes were more international, and included *Robinson Crusoe*, *Uncle Tom's Cabin* and *Don Quixote*. Another favourite was the Bible in which he hoped to find justification for his anti-Semitism. He enjoyed the music of Beethoven and Weber, but his greatest love remained opera, particularly the works of Richard Wagner. In Vienna, Hitler had enjoyed the theatre. Now he was a fan of the movies too, including American movies and the Hollywood star, Greta Garbo. He continued to be interested in art and in 1933 laid the foundation stone for the Munich House of German Art. However, when he saw the first selection of paintings he was so furious with the modern art he saw there that he threatened to shut the exhibition down. Hitler believed that modern art was evidence of a decadent Western world. In 1938 he passed a law that banned modern art from being exhibited.

## Culture and Nazi Germany

Behind his back some of his Nazi colleagues joked about Hitler's interest in culture and the arts, but Hitler recognized that art and politics went hand in hand.

He realized that the arts could influence people so it was important that access to the arts was strictly controlled. For example, in 1933, he ordered the mass burning of Jewish, communist and gay-authored books. Later in the same year, the Nazis set up the Reich Cultural Chamber, a building with separate chambers for literature, theatre, music, fine art and films. The Nazis also tried to

▲ *Paintings of the perfect Aryan family were acceptable in Nazi Germany. This oil painting by Wilhelm Haller shows a blond German couple with their five children. Rolling hills in the background complete the idealized vision.*

bring high culture to the people. In factories, workers would have to take breaks from the production line in order to listen to orchestras playing rousing German classical music.

## Body matters

When most people think of Adolf Hitler they often picture his hard expression and his stiff demeanour, and they think of his lust for power and propensity for evil. In many ways it's easy to forget that he was a real person who felt pain and suffered from illness. In fact, from the middle of the 1930s Hitler was seeing more and more of doctors and

▼ *Almost human: Hitler relaxes at his Berghof mountain retreat. This photograph was probably taken by Eva Braun.*

psychiatrists, and relying upon greater and greater doses of powerful drugs to keep himself going.

Some of Hitler's ailments, such as high blood pressure, eczema and stomach problems, could be clearly put down to stress, made worse by his bad temper. Other problems could be blamed on his diet. Since Geli's death he had become a vegetarian, but this made his stomach problems and flatulence worse. Hitler also had a sweet tooth and as he got older he was inclined to put on weight. Hitler feared death, but it only worried him because he believed he had so much to achieve and that he might run out of time. In 1935, when his voice became hoarse, he was afraid that he might have cancer of the throat. It turned out that the small growth on his larynx wasn't malignant. The operation to remove it was a success – but like so much of his private life, it was kept secret.

## In the hands of fate

As extraordinary as it might seem, Hitler, the all-powerful dictator, also believed in fate, and dabbled in astrology. In 1933, he sought help from one of Europe's leading astrologers, Erik Jan Hanussen. Hitler

▲ *Almost mad: Hitler rehearsed for his speeches as if he were an actor. It's easy to believe there was insanity in Hitler's family when you see pictures like this.*

wanted to find out if the famous astrologer could advise him about his future. Hanussen more or less told him that he would rise to power. We don't know if Hitler believed the astrologer's predictions, but it's interesting that he was prepared to listen to them.

# Foreign policy: 1933–1940

**Hitler's greatest ambition was to make all German-speaking people part of the Reich.**

▶ *German troops march into Vienna in spring 1938. Nazi Germany was on the road to war.*

Many years before, Hitler had also written about Germany's lack of living space (*Lebensraum*) in *Mein Kampf*. He believed that the country could only be secure if it had more land and space. "The greater the quantity of space at the disposal of a people, the greater its natural protection," he wrote. So we know that expansion into foreign territories was always in his mind.

The aims of Hitler's foreign policy are still disputed by the historians and experts on Nazi Germany. Hitler's first goal was to dismantle the Treaty of Versailles, but what did he intend to do next? Did he aim to take over Europe and create a German empire, or was he looking towards Russia and its collapse? Some people assume he was an opportunist who was just aiming to make Germany great and implemented his aims one step at a time, as and when suitable chances arose.

## Preparation for war

In the 1930s, ordinary people in Germany craved peace. But as early as 1933, Hitler was preparing for war. Under the rearmament programme, Germany had been building its military machine, and in 1935, in direct contravention of the Treaty of Versailles, conscription had been reintroduced. In 1934 Hitler had signed a ten-year non-aggression pact with Poland, but he had no intention of keeping the peace. It was probably a diversionary tactic that helped him to persuade France and Britain that rearmament and conscription weren't acts of aggression: that he was merely restoring Germany's military honour. He must have convinced them, as Britain signed a naval pact with Germany allowing them to rebuild their navy – up to one-third of the size of the Royal Navy. This would prove to be just one of the many occasions when Hitler managed to blind his enemies with a diplomatic smokescreen.

## Occupation of the Rhineland

By the middle of the 1930s, new wars threatened to disturb the peace in Europe. Hitler waited for the right moment for Germany to enter the arena. In 1935–6 when the Italian Fascist dictator Benito Mussolini invaded Ethiopia, Hitler noted that France and Britain failed to rein Italy in with economic sanctions. He decided the time was right to strike a blow of his own. In March 1936, Hitler ordered his German troops to occupy the demilitarized Rhineland. It was another challenge to the Treaty of Versailles but Hitler predicted, correctly, that France and Britain wouldn't do anything about it.

## Invasion of Austria

Later in 1936, when the Spanish Civil War broke out, Hitler forged an alliance with Mussolini. In the same year, Hitler signed a pact with Japan to fight the spread of communism. Within a short time, Hitler had made new allies. In 1938 when he took control of Germany's armed forces he was prepared for his next

### Lebensraum

"The aim of German policy is to make sure to preserve the racial Community and to enlarge it. It is therefore a question of (living) space..."
Hitler on 5 November 1937 speaking in the Chancellery.

▲ *Fascist leaders unite. Hitler pays a state visit to Italy in May 1938. The pact between the two dictators Mussolini (left) and Hitler lasted until 1943.*

move – to unite the German-speaking people of his native Austria with Germany. In March 1938, after months of threats, Hitler ordered German troops to enter Vienna, in Austria. Within days, Hitler was able to lead a triumphant celebration – a motorcade – from Munich to Vienna. It would be an emotional homecoming at which Hitler proclaimed an *Anschluss*, or union, between Germany and Austria. He later told his valet, "It is fate, Linge. I am destined to be the

Führer who will bring all Germans into the Greater German Reich."

## Claiming the Sudetenland

Hitler planned his next campaign carefully. This time he aimed to reclaim a German-speaking region of Czechoslovakia called the Sudetenland. In September 1938, he met with the British and French Prime Ministers, Neville Chamberlain and Edouard Daladier, and the Czechoslovak President, Eduard Benes. France and Britain were eager to avoid war. Eventually an agreement was signed whereby 18,400 sq km of Czechoslovak territory were given to Hitler. Hitler promised that this would be his last demand. But on 14 March 1939, Germany invaded the rest of Czechoslovakia. The era of appeasement was finally at an end.

## Final steps to war

In January 1939, Hitler turned his attention to Poland. He began by demanding that the Poles hand over the corridor of land that separated East Prussia from the rest of Germany. The land was important to Poland as it was

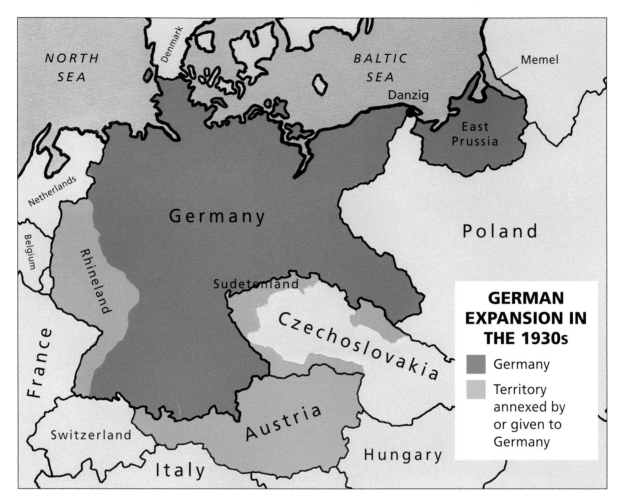

NORTH SEA

Denmark

BALTIC SEA

Memel

Danzig

East Prussia

Netherlands

Germany

Poland

Belgium

Rhineland

Sudetenland

Czechoslovakia

France

**GERMAN EXPANSION IN THE 1930s**

Germany

Territory annexed by or given to Germany

Switzerland

Austria

Hungary

Italy

the country's only access to the sea and it contained the valuable seaport of Danzig. Fearing that Hitler would use force, Britain and France guaranteed Poland military protection. Meanwhile, Hitler was making alliances of his own. In May 1939 he signed a pact with Mussolini (the "Pact of Steel"), in which they agreed to support each other in any future war.

Then, in August 1939, he made a non-aggression pact with the communist Soviet leader, Joseph Stalin. Hitler's hatred of communists was well known so the pact came as a shock to France and Britain, but Hitler believed that with the Soviets on his side, France and Britain wouldn't help the Poles. It was to prove a terrible miscalculation.

## Poland is blitzed

Hitler planned surprise attacks on Poland using concentrated firepower over short bursts of time. This was a tactic known as Blitzkrieg (lightning war). On 1 September 1939, the blitzkrieg on Poland began. Two days later, when Britain and France declared war on Germany, war between the European superpowers had begun. Hitler had a genuine admiration for the British. He had hoped that they could be talked out of war. But when he realized that he would have go to war with them, he was resolute. In a speech on 1 September, he told the Reichstag, "I will carry on this fight, no matter against whom, until the safety of the Reich and its rights are secured! From this moment,

my whole life shall belong more than ever to my people. I now want to be nothing but the first soldier of the German Reich. Therefore, I have once again put on that uniform which was always so sacred to and dear to me. I shall not

▶ This cartoon from 1939 makes fun of the alliance between Hitler and Stalin.

take it off until after the victory – or I shall not live to see the end!"

On 17 September the Soviets entered Poland from the east. The attack on Poland happened too quickly for the Allies to help, and defeat for the Poles came about within six weeks. Believing he should lead by example, Hitler stayed near the action and arrived at the front line each day, armed with his pistol and whip, to inspect proceedings. In Germany the news of another war hit people hard. But they were living in a dictatorship and criticism was forbidden. Nobody was allowed to listen to foreign radio transmissions and, within Germany, Nazi propaganda presented the war as a necessary evil.

## Days of victory

Hitler then turned his attentions to the West. With massive numbers of aircraft, tanks and lorries the German war machine would prove to be too powerful for other European countries to be able to put up much resistance. In April 1940, Germany conquered Denmark and Norway. Hitler's sights were now set on France. The French had built a line of defence called the "Maginot Line" along their border with Germany. Meanwhile the British had dug trenches at Lille, near the Belgian border. On 10 May 1940, the Germans found an easy way around the Allies' defences. First, they began attacking northern Belgium and the Netherlands by air. So the Allies responded by advancing north, leaving the south of the Maginot Line, near Sedan, open to the German tanks. The German war machine advanced rapidly. By 23 May 1940, the Germans were a few miles from Dunkirk on the English Channel, and the British forces were retreating. It was at this point (against the wishes of his generals), that Hitler ordered his tanks to stop. Invasion of Britain had seemed inevitable, yet Hitler's orders enabled 338,000 British servicemen to escape from Dunkirk. It seems that Hitler had hoped that he could still make peace with Britain. But Britain was in no mood to make peace with Nazi Germany, and its new prime minister Winston Churchill had promised his country victory at any cost.

▶ *Hitler enjoys a moment of triumph in front of the Eiffel Tower in Paris, soon after the German invasion of France in June 1940. Hitler was "fascinated" by Paris.*

# War on all fronts: 1940–1942

On 22 June 1940, the French armistice was signed at Compiègne. This was poignant, because Germany had surrendered here at the end of World War One. The French were now under Nazi rule.

Hitler was in a triumphant mood and spoke of destroying everything that reminded the world of the shame of 1918. He later travelled to Paris, a city that had always fascinated him, and visited the Eiffel Tower and Napoleon's Tomb. With its fine architecture and art, Paris was everything he had always imagined and he talked about making Berlin more beautiful than the French capital one day.

## Blitzing Britain

Hitler's confidence in his own judgement and military planning was on a new high. He became less likely to listen to the advice of his generals and more likely to issue counteractive orders. In July 1940, Hitler spoke to the Reichstag of his hope for peace with Britain: "Mr Churchill ought perhaps, for once, to believe me when I prophesy that a great empire will be destroyed – an empire which it was never my intention to destroy or even to harm…" Hitler's threats did nothing to dent Churchill's iron will and Hitler was forced to continue to wage war against Britain.

So, in August 1940, Hitler planned to wipe out the Royal Air Force and make a naval invasion of Britain. On 13 August 1940, German bombers attacked British airbases; in September they blitzed London. Hitler was convinced that the British would surrender, but despite high civilian casualties and heavy losses to the RAF, Britain soldiered on. Hitler felt compelled to change tactics, and, once more, he halted an offensive which might have won him the war. Instead he looked towards the defeat of the USSR in a campaign named "Operation Barbarossa". A year earlier, Hitler and Stalin had

▲ Hitler and Mussolini discuss tactics for the Eastern
Front with Field Marshal Wilhelm Keitel (background)
and General Alfred Jödl (right).

signed a non-aggression pact, but Hitler
had never really trusted Stalin. He
believed the threat of Soviet intervention
against Germany kept Britain in the war.
If Germany defeated the USSR then
Britain would be forced to surrender.

## The desert war

In Britain, Churchill was doing his best
to get the United States to join forces
with the Allies against the Nazis, and by
September a deal had been struck
whereby the USA provided Britain with
warships. Ever mindful of possible
American intervention against Germany
in the war, Hitler had strengthened his
alliance with Italy and Japan, with the

Tripartite Pact. But this brought him new problems. Italy had been fighting against the British in North Africa, so in January 1941 Hitler was forced to send one of his finest generals – Field Marshal Erwin Rommel – to Africa to help the Italians. By April 1941, Rommel had driven the British back towards Egypt. Germany appeared victorious, yet in undertaking a war in the desert Hitler had been forced to take men and military machinery away from the war in Europe.

## Operation Barbarossa

In June 1941, as the war in Africa progressed, Hitler launched Operation Barbarossa against the USSR. Stalin was unprepared and by early July Germany had advanced deep into the USSR. However, Hitler was about to make another decision that would cost him dearly. In the past, the success of blitzkrieg had been based on speed and concentration of military power. Now Hitler planned to divide the German forces into three, and make a three-pronged attack upon Leningrad, Moscow and the Ukraine. Spread so thinly, the German army was not easily able to tackle the large numbers of Soviet troops,

nor was it equipped for the bitterly cold Russian winter. As the rains came down, the roads were turned to mud so thick that the German tanks couldn't move. By November, snow and freezing conditions meant that German troops were trapped 100 kilometres outside Moscow. Dressed in light summer uniforms, many German soldiers perished in the snow. Hitler insisted that all his men fight on: "There must be no withdrawal ... The enemy will gradually bleed themselves to death with their attack."

## War with the USA

By December 1941 it was clear that the war in the USSR wasn't going to plan. Nor were the British any nearer to surrender. That same month, Hitler appointed himself Commander-in-Chief of the army – the generals who secretly called him the "bohemian corporal" would now have even less influence over his decisions. The Japanese attacked Pearl Harbor on 7 December 1941, and Hitler declared war on the USA on 11 December. By acting against the wishes of many of his army generals he was taking his country to war with the largest industrial nation in the world.

## The "New Order"

By 1942 victory in Europe was by no means certain, yet Hitler's vision of a German empire was taking shape. He'd envisioned a great state, a "New Order", with all Jews removed. After taking over Austria, Czechoslovakia and Poland there were an estimated four million Jews living under Nazi rule. Within the Soviet Union, which Hitler still believed he would conquer, there were millions more. How did Hitler plan to deal with the "Jewish problem" there?

## The "Jewish Problem"

As in Germany and Nazi-occupied countries, what happened in Poland revealed the brutal treatment that the Nazis were capable of inflicting. In 1939, at the start of occupation, Jews there were forced to wear a yellow Star of David to identify them. They suffered humiliation and terror, and, in many instances, had their homes and businesses confiscated. Eventually, they were herded into ghettos or concentration camps to live in appalling conditions with no heat or food, while being forced to work for the Nazis. Many people died from malnutrition or disease, while others were killed by firing squads. It soon became obvious to Hitler that this wasn't an efficient method for getting rid of the large number of Jews throughout Europe. At one point Hitler showed an interest in setting up a "devil's island" for the Jews on the island of Madagascar. Then, in July 1941, he had handed responsibility for the Jewish problem to Heinrich Himmler and Reinhard Heydrich.

## The "Final Solution"

In 1939, Hitler had already demonstrated the lengths he'd go to "cleanse" Germany of those he considered to be imperfect or non-Aryan stock, when he had ordered a euthanasia programme. On this occasion over 80,000 disabled, mentally ill, criminal or long-term unemployed Germans had been killed by lethal injection or carbon monoxide gas. A public outcry had brought that programme to an end but now Heydrich and Himmler planned the "final solution", a term used by the Nazis to describe the mass genocide of Jews, communists and other "undesirables", such as gypsies and homosexuals. Although Hitler distanced himself from the final solution, there is little doubt that it was acted out under his orders. For years he had spoken out against the Jews and in 1942 he talked of "extermination" and "elimination" of the Jews (see page 78). The details of the final solution were finalized in a conference at Wannsee, near Berlin, in January 1942. Heydrich read out a report that detailed how Jews capable of work would be employed on behalf of the German war effort. While most of those were expected to work themselves to death, other Jews would be put to death by an "appropriate treatment".

## The death camps

The "treatment" that Heydrich proposed was death by poison gas. The Nazis quickly set up concentration camps throughout Nazi-occupied Europe, the first of which was at Chelmo in Poland. Jews and other victims were rounded up from occupied territories and taken by train to the camps. At the camps the fittest were selected to work, while young children, older people and those considered unfit, were taken away to be gassed. By 1942, some Nazi concentration camps had evolved into highly efficient death camps run by the SS. Prisoners

▲ In Germany and Nazi-occupied countries, Jews were forced to wear a yellow star so that they would stand out from their non-Jewish neighbours.

▼ Another Nazi measure to isolate Jews was to make them carry Jewish identity cards which bore their photograph and fingerprints.

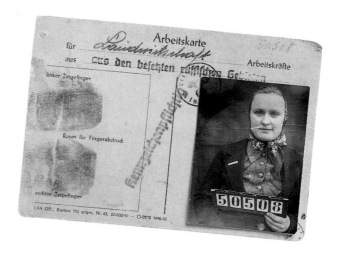

▲ The Warsaw Ghetto had been created by the Nazis in 1940 soon after the invasion of Poland. By 1943 most of the Jews in the Ghetto had been rounded up and taken to concentration camps.

were herded into gas chambers disguised as shower blocks. Once the victims were inside the chamber, the doors were locked and lethal Zyklon-B or carbon monoxide was pumped in. Afterwards, the bodies were searched for jewellery and other valuables such as gold teeth. The corpses were later burned in furnaces that blazed day and night, destroying the evidence of such an evil crime. The concentration camps harboured other Nazi attrocities too. At Auschwitz, Dr. Josef Mengele, also known as "the Angel of Death", selected people he wanted to perform medical and surgical experiments upon. In other camps, starving people were forced to work until they were too weak to carry on and were exterminated. Today, historians argue about Hitler's role in the Holocaust. A few suggest that there is a lack of evidence against him. But most say that his speeches make his involvement apparent. They claim he was a manipulative politician who realized that the mass murder of millions would shock and appal too many people, and, to survive as leader, he had to distance himself from such events.

## Hitler's plans for the Jews

"One must act radically. When one pulls out a tooth, one does it with a single tug, and the pain quickly goes away. The Jews must clear out of Europe. It's the Jews who prevent everything. When I think about it, I realize that I'm extraordinarily humane. At the time of the rules of the Popes the Jews were mistreated in Rome. Until 1830, eight Jews mounted on donkeys were led once a year through the streets of Rome. For my part, I restrict myself to telling them they must go away . . . if they refuse to go voluntarily I see no other solution than extermination."
Hitler, in the presence of Himmler, at lunch on 23 January 1942.
quoted in *Hitler* by John Tolland

"If the international Jewish financiers in and outside Europe should succeed in plunging the nations once more into a world war, then the result will not be the Bolshevizing of the earth, and thus a victory of Jewry, but the annihilation of the Jewish race in Europe."
Hitler, quoted in *New Perspectives: The Holocaust* by R.G. Grant

▶ *In the barracks at camps such as Buchenwald (shown here) disease was rampant. The seventh figure from left in the second row (with face partially hidden) is the Jewish writer Elie Wiesel.*

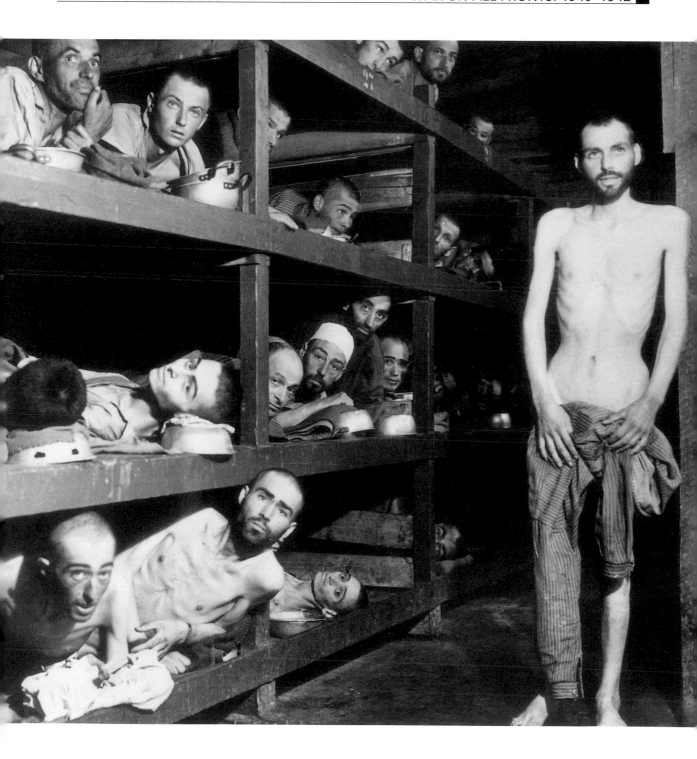

# The misfortunes of war

**The year 1942 would prove to be a turning point for the warlord Adolf Hitler. The German Reich was at its greatest extent, yet by declaring war on the USA Hitler had caused a world war – a war that would be long and costly.**

United in their mission to crush the Nazis, the American, British and Soviet allies worked closely together on strategy, while the Germans, Italians and Japanese did not work together as effectively.

## Germany is attacked

In May 1942 the Allies began bombing major German cities. For the next three years, bombs rained down on Essen, Düsseldorf and Cologne. In a series of day and night raids thousands of civilians were terrorized and killed. For the first time, ordinary Germans were experiencing the horror of war on their own doorsteps. They had not expected death on this scale and morale plummeted. As usual Hitler and his propaganda machine tried to convince

them that waging war was the right thing to do. In speeches he claimed that the American President, Franklin D Roosevelt, was mentally ill and a "pawn" of the Jews. He said that Germany would save Europe from Bolshevism. He also favourably compared himself to another warlord, Napoleon: "We have mastered destiny which broke another man a hundred and thirty years ago," he told the Reichstag in early 1942.

## The Soviet offensive

German soldiers had held out throughout the cold Soviet winter of 1941–1942, and by spring 1942 Hitler was considering his next move against the USSR. Against the advice of his generals, Hitler was planning a two-pronged attack on the industrial city of Stalingrad on the Volga,

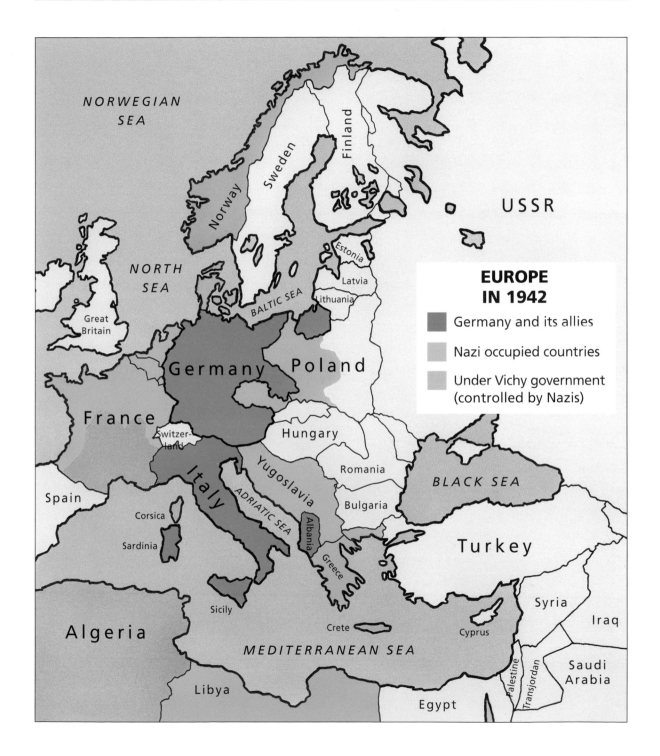

**EUROPE IN 1942**

Germany and its allies

Nazi occupied countries

Under Vichy government
(controlled by Nazis)

NORWEGIAN SEA

Norway

Sweden

Finland

USSR

NORTH SEA

Great Britain

BALTIC SEA

Estonia

Latvia

Lithuania

Germany

Poland

France

Switzer-land

Hungary

Italy

Yugoslavia

Romania

Spain

ADRIATIC SEA

Bulgaria

BLACK SEA

Corsica

Albania

Turkey

Sardinia

Greece

Algeria

Sicily

Crete

Cyprus

Syria

Iraq

MEDITERRANEAN SEA

Palestine

Transjordan

Saudi Arabia

Libya

Egypt

and the Soviet oilfields of the Caucasus. It was an overly ambitious plan that would mean dividing his forces between two fronts. It was the same mistake he had made during Operation Barbarossa, yet if anybody tried to reason with him, Hitler's temper flared and he lashed out unreasonably. Around this time, his health began to decline seriously and he suffered with pounding headaches and hours of sleeplessness. He now spent most of his time hidden away in the forests at Rastenburg in East Prussia at his headquarters, the *Wolfsschanze*, or Wolf's Lair, and people rarely saw him.

The Battle of Stalingrad started on 19 August 1942. Hitler was confident that seizing Stalingrad, and then the Caucasus, would be easy. His confidence had been boosted by German successes in the USSR and North Africa. In the past two months thousands of Soviet troops had been killed in battles at Kharkov and Voronezh. Meanwhile, in Africa, Rommel had driven the British back from their stronghold of Tobruk and was advancing towards El Alamein. Hitler had reason to feel triumphant – but the tide was about to turn against the Nazis and in favour of the Allies.

## The turning tide

By concentrating on the war in Europe, Hitler had neglected the war in North Africa. Throughout this offensive Rommel had been outnumbered by enemy soldiers and military machinery, yet he'd still managed to break through the British defences. In early November 1942, Rommel's luck ran out and the Germans were defeated at El Alamein. Rommel contacted Hitler and requested a retreat, but Hitler was adamant that he should hold out: "The choice is victory or death," he told him. Rommel acted against his Führer's wishes and withdrew his men, although historians aren't sure whether he had actually received Hitler's orders or not.

Defeat in Africa was followed by setbacks at Stalingrad. By 18 November 1942, the Soviet army had managed to surround the German Sixth Army. General Friedrich Paulus had asked Hitler if his men could retreat but once again Hitler refused, and told his generals to "fight to the last man". Paulus's men managed to hold out for two more months, but during that time, 146,000

▶ *German troops surrender at Stalingrad on 31 January 1943 and are taken prisoner.*

soldiers were killed. On 2 February 1943, against Hitler's wishes, Paulus surrendered and 90,000 men were made prisoners of war. Hitler was furious; he believed Paulus should have shot himself rather than surrender.

Events at El Alamein and Stalingrad shook Hitler. He became depressed and unreasonable, mainly choosing to eat and sleep at the Wolf's Lair with only his dog, Blondi, for company. He no longer listened to music, and on the rare occasions he had visitors he talked long into the night about his early years in Vienna, or about history, rather than face the reality of the war he was losing. Throughout Germany people reacted to the war news with shock and dismay. Hitler had assured them of victory, yet Germany had been beaten. He'd promised them better lives, but the war was draining the economy. In Berlin there were three days of mourning for the missing soldiers. With theatres and bars closed, the mood was grim – and deteriorating fast. More than ever the

◀ A Nazi propaganda poster urges German civilians to do their bit for the war effort. The poster reads: "Just as we fight so will you work for victory!"

Nazi propaganda machine was needed to cast its spell over ordinary Germans.

## "Total War"

By 1943 Goebbels had become the pubic mouthpiece for Hitler. In fact, the Führer only delivered two more speeches in public. On 18 February 1943, Goebbels launched the "Total War" campaign. The aim was to raise the same "Dunkirk spirit" in the Germans that had been observed in the British public. The message was that Germany could still win the war if everybody pulled together for the war effort. In the past Hitler had believed that a woman's place was in the home; now women were needed in the factories. By 1944 Germany's 14.9 million women workers made up over half of Germany's native workforce. The Hitler Youth had been set up to educate the children. Now those children aged between 10 and 15 were expected to volunteer for war work such as farm work or collecting rags. From all over Nazi-occupied territories more and more people were drafted in to man the munitions factories. Many of these non-German speaking people came unwillingly, and were treated little better than slaves. During the years 1941–1944 war production increased by 230 per cent, but the Total War campaign had come too late to save Germany.

## Operation Gomorrah

The German people were told that production was increasing, yet everywhere they looked they saw destruction. The saturation bombing of German cities and industrial areas had been devised by the Allies to halt industrial production, and cause such panic in the population that they would plead for peace. From March to July 1943, the RAF targeted the Ruhr's industrial towns, but in July and August of that year the Allies turned on Hamburg. Operation Gomorrah, as it was aptly called, began with intensive air raids; for over a week bombs rained down on the city, with the RAF bombing it by night and the American Air Force (USAAF) bombing it during the day. The blazing inferno destroyed nearly three-quarters of Hamburg. Over 44,600 people were killed and approximately 1.2 million people fled or were evacuated. At last, the Allies had found a way to defeat Germany. That autumn they targeted Berlin in the hope that this might crush Germany

completely. Again the attack was relentless and over half the city's homes were flattened, but the war was far from over.

## At the Wolf's Lair

By 1943, Hitler divided his time between the Berghof and the Wolf's Lair. By now his tempers were so bad that his staff were frightened to tell him any bad news. Instead there was an atmosphere of enforced pleasantness, with Hitler following a daily schedule that included a mid-morning briefing before entertaining his waiting guests. Hitler refused to visit the bombed-out cities; he left that job to Goebbels. When he talked of the air raids he became angry and accused certain British commanders of being part-Jewish. Most evenings he refused to sleep until he knew that all enemy planes had left Germany's airspace. As the great cities of Germany burned, Hitler was enjoying himself making new town plans and models of cities such as Munich and Linz. From now on his detachment from reality seemed to grow more and more evident.

▼ *The Allies bring death and destruction to the streets of Hamburg during Operation Gomorrah in July 1943.*

# Final collapse of the Nazis

**By 1943 many of Hitler's generals doubted that Germany could win the war. But Hitler believed that Germany could not be seen to falter, and talked of renewed efforts against the Soviets.**

This time Hitler planned an attack on the Eastern front at Kursk. The offensive was a gamble, but Hitler promised his forces up-to-date equipment and more men to fight this difficult campaign. By July the new tanks hadn't arrived, but a million back-up soldiers had poured into the region. Hitler felt uneasy about the attack and postponed it three times. Unwittingly, he had given the Soviets enough time to regroup and build up their defences. On 4 July 1943, more than 6,000 tanks clashed in what would be the biggest tank battle of the entire war. Over 70,000 Germans were killed and 1,500 tanks were lost. Previously Hitler had always told his soldiers to stand up and fight to the death, but on 13 July 1943, he ordered his men to stop fighting. Germany had lost the Battle of Kursk and it had been Hitler's own fault. From now on, all Germany's efforts in the East would amount to one long retreat.

## A fight to the end

By the end of July 1943, against all odds, Hitler still believed he could win the war. But the Battle of Kursk had been a disaster. Then, on 10 July 1943, news reached him that the Allies had landed in Sicily. By 25 July, Hitler's closest ally, Mussolini, had been arrested and the new Italian government looked set for peace talks with the Allies. To add to the humiliation, American and British bombers had almost destroyed Hamburg. Yet still Hitler wasn't ready to admit defeat and he ordered the evacuation of 60,000 German troops from Sicily. In a

▼ *A wrecked German tank and dead soldier after the Battle of Kursk in 1943.*

speech broadcast on 10 September 1943, he told his country: "My right to believe unconditionally in success is founded not only on my own life but also on the destiny of our people." Within days the Germans had seized Rome, and Hitler had arranged a daring mission to rescue Mussolini.

In October 1943, the new Italian government declared war on Germany; however, the German occupation of Rome and northern Italy meant it would take the Allies nearly two years to fight their way through Italy. Hitler remained out of sight, hidden away at the Wolf's Lair. Christmas of 1943 was a bleak time. Hitler wanted no Christmas tree or decorations. Meanwhile, far away on the Eastern front in Russia, his troops faced another cold winter. By January 1944, the Germans had been pushed back from Leningrad and the Soviets had claimed back much of the Ukraine. The picture was gloomy but Hitler still believed Germany should fight to the last man. His health was growing steadily worse, but his spirits were lifted by the successful development of the V-1 rocket. He believed that these flying bombs targeted at mainland Britain could win the war for

Germany. It was a glimmer of hope, as all his other plans for a victorious Germany crumbled about him.

## The D-Day Landings

On 6 June 1944 Hitler awoke late to the news that the Allies had landed on the north coast of France at Normandy. It was the beginning of the D-Day landings. Hitler's generals had heard about the invasion a few hours earlier but had been too scared to rouse the Führer. Hitler's reaction was strange; one moment he was angry, the next he was chuckling with excitement at the thought of being face to face with his enemies. In truth, he didn't believe this was the real invasion; he had expected the Allies to land at Calais. Once again, he had misjudged the situation and given his military commanders no clear indication as to how they should proceed. Within weeks, over one million Allied troops and huge amounts of ammunition had been landed on the beaches of northern France. The Germans were outnumbered on land, at sea and by air; the situation looked

▶ *Hitler was still asleep when American troops came ashore at Omaha Beach in Normandy on 6 June 1944.*

hopeless. Rommel wrote to Hitler suggesting it was time to stop fighting, but Hitler still believed that with the V-1 rocket the British would surrender. Later that month, Germany launched its deadly V-2 rockets at London and other major cities in Britain. Within a few weeks 6,139 British civilians had been killed, but in France, the Allies fought on.

## The July bomb plot

Hitler was no stranger to attempts on his life. Since 1938 there had been at least five plots to kill him, but in July 1944 one man got close to ending the Führer's life. For months, senior members of the German army had realized that a German victory looked very unlikely, and that Hitler would never consider peace talks. A group of conspirators headed by a respected war hero called Colonel Claus von Stauffenberg, believed that the only way to save Germany was to assassinate Hitler and stage a coup. On the morning of 20 July 1944, Stauffenberg had managed to smuggle two briefcases containing bombs into the Wolf's Lair

▶ Hitler shows Mussolini the damage caused by the bomb at the Wolf's Lair. Both men were deeply shocked but Hitler said he felt "new courage".

and had hidden them under a map table. When Stauffenberg left the room, the fuse had been set and Hitler was just metres away from the activated bomb.

As Stauffenberg reached his getaway car, he heard the explosion. Convinced that he had killed Hitler, Stauffenberg escaped to Berlin. In fact, Hitler managed to walk away from the blast with only a few cuts and bruises, perforated eardrums and a slight limp.

He later told his doctor: "I am invulnerable, I am immortal." More than ever, he believed that he'd been specially chosen to continue the fight for Germany.

Those that had conspired against the Führer paid the highest price. Stauffenberg and the other senior army officers in the conspiracy were arrested and shot. A further 5,000 suspects were executed. Not even the outstanding commander Rommel was spared. Although there was no evidence he was involved in the plot, he'd been a close friend of many of the conspirators. Hitler gave him a choice of facing trial or taking poison. On 14 October 1944, Rommel committed suicide.

## Hitler's health

Anyone who saw Hitler at this time was shocked to notice that he had aged dramatically and his health had deteriorated terribly. His right hand now shook so much that he could no longer shave himself, and he'd even started to forget people's names. Historians now believe that he might have had the first symptoms of Parkinson's Disease, a neurological disorder which can cause dementia. He was also taking a cocktail of drugs to help him sleep and, in turn, other drugs to keep him awake. Perhaps these facts can explain Hitler's steadfast but, by this time, utterly deluded belief that Germany could still defeat the Allies and win the war.

## End of the dream

On 25 August 1944, after four years of Nazi occupation, the Allies liberated Paris. From there they advanced through France, while Soviet troops swooped through Romania and into Poland. As his enemies drew closer, Hitler's thoughts turned to the death camps. By August 1944, it is estimated that six million people, mainly Jews, had been murdered in the Nazis' death camps. It was now time for a massive cover-up. Hitler told Himmler to begin shutting down all the camps – except Auschwitz as he believed there was still work to do there – and ordered that all the buildings and documents relating to the camps should be destroyed.

## The last stand begins

On 16 December 1944, Germany made a last stand, with a surprise attack against the Allies via the Ardennes in Belgium. "No one can last forever. We can't, the other side can't," Hitler said. "It's merely a question of who can stand it longer. The one who must hold out longer is the one who's got everything at stake." Despite early success, the Germans withdrew in January 1945. An earlier retreat might have saved some of the 100,000 German casualties, or the 600 tanks and 1,600 aircraft that were lost, but Hitler insisted that his men fight on. Later in January, when the Soviets took Warsaw and part of East Prussia, Hitler had already returned to Berlin. While his soldiers fell, he hid away in a concrete bunker underneath the Chancellery taking comfort only in the company of his dogs.

# The last months

**Hitler claimed he moved to the bunker at the Chancellery to get some sleep during the air raids.**

In fact his final days, lived out in a few darkened rooms, probably passed like a nightmare, as his existence now hung between life and death. He made few appearances above ground again, and on 30 January 1945, exactly twelve years to the day since he became Chancellor, he made his last radio broadcast. He had nothing new to say; Germany had heard it all before. He urged his people to do their duty to the last and rid the world of Jews and communists. "However grave the crisis may be at the moment," he told them, "it will, despite everything, finally be mastered by our unalterable will, by our readiness for sacrifice and by our abilities." In truth, Germany had already given everything it could.

▶ *In April 1945 the Allies began liberating the Nazi concentration camps. The experience was often likened to a living nightmare. These ravaged and starving inmates from Dachau would be some of the lucky ones.*

## The final word

By the end of January 1945, the Soviets had crossed the Oder River, the last natural barrier before Berlin. As American bombers rained bombs down on the German capital, leading Nazis believed that time was running out. During one raid the Chancellery itself was hit so badly that the lines of communication, the power and water supply were all destroyed. Yet Hitler remained defiant and began dictating his final interpretation of the war to his secretary Martin Bormann. He wanted to record how close he had come to winning, and he wanted to apportion blame for the mistakes that had brought about his downfall. He pointed the finger at the British, who he claimed could have ended the war in 1941 if they had surrendered. He ranted about Jews and communists, and found a way to blame everybody except himself. His companions in the bunker were startled by his detachment from reality. Even as the bombs roared overhead, Hitler still dreamed of victory.

▶ *Dresden, the seventh largest city in Germany, was virtually destroyed by Allied air raids. On 13 February 1945 the blazing city was visible from 320 km away.*

## Desperation and destruction

Between 13 and 15 February 1945, the Allies bombed Dresden. A massive firestorm destroyed much of the city and reports suggested that as many as 25,000 civilians had been killed, while 35,000 were missing. Hitler was angry, but ruled out executing prisoners of war in retaliation. By 3 March 1945, when American and British troops crossed the Rhine, his mood was less forgiving. But this time, he turned against his own people: "If the war is lost, the German nation will also perish," Hitler told his armaments minister, Albert Speer. "There is no need to take into consideration the basic requirements of the people … Those who will remain after the battle are those who are inferior; for the good will have fallen." In the following days he ordered the destruction of anything of use to the Allies, including industrial sites, bridges, waterways and energy sources. Hitler had always demanded loyalty from his people but ultimately he never returned it to them. Although retreating German troops did do some damage, Speer managed to prevent any large-scale destruction.

## The enemy at the door

In February 1945, Eva Braun had joined Hitler in the bunker. Her devotion touched him, but his moods continued to swing from high to low. On 12 April, his spirits were raised considerably at the news of President Roosevelt's death. Perhaps this was a turning point? A few days later, when he heard that Soviet troops were in the suburbs of Berlin, his anger returned. The German army battled against the enemy, but the Soviets moved ever closer to the centre of Berlin. By 20 April 1945, all hope had gone, but there was a forced sense of celebration in the bunker. The occasion was Hitler's fifty-sixth birthday, and among those present were the leading Nazis: Goebbels, Goering, Himmler, Bormann and Speer. Earlier that day, Hitler had met a group of Hitler Youth volunteers. They were preparing to fight against the Soviets in a last bid to save Berlin. Meanwhile, their Führer was deciding whether he should quit Berlin for the safety of the Bavarian Alps, or die alongside them in the city they were defending.

◀ *The final humiliation: surrendered German troops march through a captured Berlin on 2 May 1945. The capital city is already in ruins and their Führer is dead.*

## The bitter end

Hitler's decision to remain in Berlin was not an act of bravery. As an ex-soldier Hitler believed there was honour in death and by 22 April 1945 he was talking about suicide. The Soviets had now surrounded the city and Hitler finally admitted that it was all over. For a while he seemed calm and emotionless, but when Goering wrote to him asking if he should assume leadership of the Reich Hitler was furious. A few days later his anger erupted again when he heard that Himmler had tried to negotiate peace.

On 29 April 1945, the news that Mussolini had been killed and strung up in Milan for all to see must have haunted Hitler. Having lost the support of his closest Nazi colleagues and with Berlin crumbling, Hitler decided to kill himself.

The atmosphere in the bunker had become gloomy and stifling, and even those who remained loyal to Hitler found his behaviour bordering on the insane. In the early hours of 29 April, Goebbels, Bormann and the other remaining occupants of the bunker gathered for the wedding ceremony of Hitler and Eva.

### The human cost of World War Two

| | Peak size of wartime population | Total armed forces | Total forces killed/missing | Total civilians wounded | Total civilians killed/missing |
|---|---|---|---|---|---|
| **Germany** | 79.4 mill | 10 mill | 3.5 mill | 2 mill | 2 mill |
| **Britain** | 47.8 mill | 4.7 mill | 420,000 | 377,000 | 70,000 |
| **USSR** | 193 mill | 20 mill | 13.6 mill | 5 mill | 7.7 mill |
| **USA** | 132 mill | 16.4 mill | 292,000 | 675,000 | Under 10 |
| **Italy** | 45.4 mill | 4.5 mill | 80,000 | 25,000 | 180,000 |
| **Japan** | 73.1 mill | 6 mill | 2.6 mill | 26,000 | 953,000 |
| **France** | 41.9 mill | 5 mill | 245,000 | 90,000 | 173,000 |

NORTH
SEA

BALTIC SEA

Königsberg
to USSR 1945

East Prussia
to Poland 1945

Pomerania
and
Silesia

Danzig to
Poland
1945

German
Federal

Republic

German

Democratic

Republic

Poland

to Poland
1945

Austria

**GERMANY AFTER
WORLD WAR II**

■ German Federal Republic

■ German Democratic Republic

■ Territory ceded to
other countries

Everyone drank champagne and Hitler reminisced about his life. The following morning he said his goodbyes to his staff and his dog Blondi who was taken away to be put down. Everybody knew what Hitler was about to do. He had even given orders about how he would like his body to be disposed of. At 3.30 p.m. that afternoon a single shot was heard. Hitler had put a bullet through his head, and Eva had taken poison. Their bodies were later taken upstairs, doused with petrol and burned – the Führer's directions had been followed to the bitter end.

On that same day Red Army soldiers waved a Soviet flag from the top of the Reichstag building. The streets below were filled with rubble, while clouds of smoke and dust filled the air. In the final battle to save their capital, 100,000 German soldiers had been killed, and perhaps as many civilians. Hitler's dream of a thousand-year Reich had brought nothing but death and destruction.

## Victory in Europe

On 7 May 1945, Germany signed an unconditional surrender, but there were many things worse than losing the war. German cities had been flattened, millions of soldiers and civilians had been killed, and Germany would lose territory and ultimately be divided into two countries – the Federal Republic in the west and the communist Democratic Republic in the east. But the greatest humiliation came when the world heard about the Nazi concentration camps. When the Allies liberated the camps, they found the people who had been lucky enough to escape death. They also found piles of corpses and other evidence. Germans were made to visit the camps to see what had happened. We'll never know how much ordinary Germans knew about the Holocaust, but the hatred and evil caused by Adolf Hitler had brought shame to all of them.

▶ *"Der Befreier Deutschlands" (The man who made Germany free) photographed at Obersalzberg in 1933.*

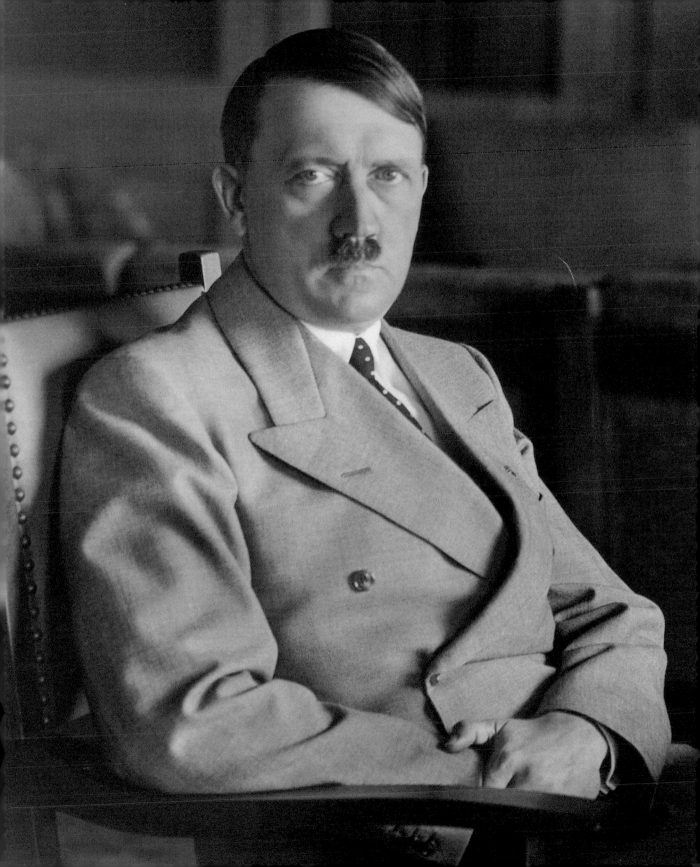

# Glossary

**abdicate** To give up the throne.

**allegiance** Loyal support.

**allies** Countries that have made an agreement to work together towards a common goal.

**anti-Semitism** Hatred of and prejudice against Jews.

**appeasement** Giving in to a potential aggressor's demands to try to prevent war.

**armistice** An end to hostilities, reached through an agreement between all sides.

**Aryans** The highest racial group of people, as defined by the Nazis.

**bohemian** An unconventional person – often used to describe artists and writers.

**Bolshevism** Russian communism – the Bolsheviks were a group of communists who seized power in Russia in 1917.

**boycott** A ban imposed on people to stop them doing certain things.

**coalition** A government made up of many different political parties.

**communism** A way of organizing a country so that the land, its housing and its industries belong to the state, and the profits are shared among everybody.

**concentration camp** A place where political prisoners were usually murdered.

**coup** A successful move – often used to describe the seizure of power in politics.

**curriculum** A programme of study.

**demilitarize** To remove armed forces from an area.

**democratic** Describes a system where the government is voted for, and is accountable to its people.

**dictator** A leader who has complete control of a country.

**elimination** To get rid of somebody or something by taking it away or killing it.

**exemplary** To be outstandingly good at something – an example to all.

**extermination** The total destruction of something or someone.

**high treason** A crime against the government or ruler of a country.

**inflation** The rate at which the cost of living goes up.

**inheritance** The property or situation, passed from one generation to the next.

**inhumane** To lack all consideration for another living thing.

**intimidation** Frightening tactics used to overpower someone.

**left-wing** The radical and socialist side of a political party and their followers.

**mark** The German unit of currency.

**munitions factory** A place where weapons and ammunition are made.

**mutiny** A rebellion against authority.

**nationalism** Extreme patriotic feelings.

**pacifist** A person who believes in peace.

**patriotism** Devotion and loyalty to one's country.

**pleural hemorrhage** A ruptured blood vessel in the lining of the lungs.

**plummet** To fall rapidly.

**Reich** A German word meaning realm.

**reparation payments** The money paid by a country to make up for the damage they caused in a war.

**rearmament** The process whereby a country builds up its army, its weapons and military machinery.

**right-wing** The conservative section of a political party and their followers.

**solidarity** Agreement to stick together between those with a common interest.

**synagogue** A Jewish place of worship.

**treaty** An official agreement between different countries.

**USSR** (Union of Soviet Socialist Republics) The Russian state which existed from 1917 to 1991.

## Further reading

*Hitler and Stalin* by Alan Bullock (HarperCollins Publishers, 1991)

*Hitler: A Study in Tyranny* by Alan Bullock (Penguin, 1980)

*Hitler and Geli* by Ronald Hayman (Bloomsbury Publishing, 1997)

*Mein Kampf (My Struggle)* by Adolf Hitler (Hutchinson, 1969)

*The Mammoth Book of How it Happened* edited by Jon E. Lewis (Robinson Publishing Ltd, 1998)

*Hitler: Diagnosis of a Destructive Prophet* by Fritz Redlich, M.D. (Oxford University Press, 1998)

*Explaining Hitler: The Search for the Origins of His Evil* by Ron Rosenbaum (Random House Group Ltd, 1998)

*Adolf Hitler*, in the Profiles series, by Richard Tames (William Heinemann, 1998)

*Hitler* by John Tolland (Wordsworth Editions Ltd, 1976)

*The World at War: The Reader's Digest Illustrated History of World War Two* (The Reader's Digest Association Ltd, 1989)

*The Third Reich,* in the Witness History Series, by David Williamson (Wayland Publishers, 1988)

*Bloomsbury Thematic Dictionary of Quotations* (Bloomsbury, 1997)

*Oxford Dictionary of Quotations* (Oxford University Press, 1999)

# Timeline

**1889 20 April:** Adolf Hitler is born at Braunau-am-Inn, Austria.

**1903** Hitler's father dies.

**1905** Hitler leaves school.

**1907** Hitler moves to Vienna; mother dies.

**1914** Hitler lives in Munich; at the outbreak of World War One he volunteers for the German army.

**1916** Hitler is wounded and recuperates in Munich.

**1918** Hitler is awarded the Iron Cross, First Class, and is temporarily blinded in a gas attack; World War One ends; an armistice is signed in France.

**1919** A constitution for Germany is drawn up at Weimar.

**28 June:** The Treaty of Versailles is signed

**September:** Hitler joins the National Socialist German Worker's Party (DAP).

**1921** The DAP is renamed the Nazi Party; Hitler becomes President of the Nazi Party.

**1922** Mussolini's "March on Rome"; he becomes prime minister of Italy.

**1923** French and Belgian troops occupy the Ruhr. The German mark collapses. Germany is hit by huge inflation.

**8–9 November:** the Putsch in Munich fails; Hitler is imprisoned at Landsberg near Munich, where he writes *Mein Kampf*.

**1924 23 December:** Hitler is released from prison.

**1925** The Nazi Party is refounded; the SS is formed; *Mein Kampf* is published; Hindenberg is elected as President of Germany.

**1927** The first Nazi mass meeting is held at Nuremberg.

**1928** The Nazi Party wins 12 seats in the German parliament (Reichstag).

**1929 29 October:** The Wall Street Crash in the USA is followed by massive unemployment in Germany.

**1930** The Nazis win 107 seats in the Reichstag.

**1931** German banks collapse; Geli Raubal dies in Hitler's apartment; Hitler stands as a candidate in the presidential elections, but is defeated by Hindenburg.

**1932 31 July:** the Nazis win 230 seats.

**November:** the Nazis win 196 seats.

**1933 30 January:** Hitler is appointed the Chancellor of Germany.

**27 February:** the Reichstag is set on fire.

**23 March:** The Enabling Law is passed, giving Hitler the powers of a dictator for four years.

**March:** The Nazis win 288 seats in the Reichstag.

**1934 30 June:** 150 SA leaders are murdered in the Night of the Long Knives.

**2 August:** President Hindenburg dies. Hitler is pronounced Chancellor and President and takes the title of Führer.

**1935 September:** The Nuremberg Laws concerning German Jews are announced.

**1936 7 March:** Hitler orders the army to occupy the Rhineland.

**September:** Four Year Plan introduced. Hitler becomes an ally of Mussolini's. The Olympic Games are held in Berlin.

**1938** Hitler becomes Commander-in-Chief of Germany's armed forces.

**12 March:** Germany takes over Austria.

**20 May:** Hitler plans an attack on Czechoslovakia. Hitler claims the Sudetenland.

**1939 March:** Germany invades Czechoslovakia.

**1939 23 May:** Hitler plans an attack on Poland.

**23 August:** Hitler signs a non-aggression pact with Stalin.

**1 September:** Germany attacks Poland.

**1940 April:** Germany occupies Norway.

**May–June:** Germany attacks France.

**June:** Italy declares war on Britain and France. Hitler decides to invade USSR.

**1941** Hitler declares war on the USA.

**1942 20 January:** The Wannsee Conference takes place.

**August:** The Battle of Stalingrad begins.

**November:** The Germans are defeated at El Alamein.

**1943 February:** The German army in Stalingrad surrenders.

**July:** British and American troops invade Sicily. Italy surrenders to the Allies.

**1944 6 June:** The D-Day landings occur.

**20 July:** The plot to murder Hitler fails.

**1945 30 January:** Hitler makes his last broadcast to his people.

**30 April:** Hitler commits suicide.

**7 May:** All German forces surrender.

**8 May:** VE (Victory in Europe) Day takes place. End of the war in Europe.

# Index

Page numbers in italics are pictures or maps.